Our Co[illegible]
Ground

a College anthology

With a foreword by HRH, the Prince of Wales,
President of The Royal Agricultural College

Edited by Peter Brooks and Lorna Parker

Illustrations by Abigail Portus

The Royal Agricultural College

Silverdart Publishing

MMXI

Published by Silverdart Publishing, London
in association with
The Royal Agricultural College, Cirencester

First edition – published privately 2010
Second edition – 2011

ISBN 978-0-9554581-6-3

Printed in Great Britain by the MPG Books Group,
Bodmin and King's Lynn.
Text pages on 100% recycled paper, cover part-recycled.

The Royal Agricultural College
Stroud Road, Cirencester,
Glos, GL7 6JS
Tel: 01285 652531
www.rac.ac.uk

Silverdart Publishing
211 Linton House,
164-180 Union Street, London SE1 0LH
Tel: 020 7928 7770
www.silverdart.co.uk

FOREWORD

For many people, no other medium can capture the glorious sensation of agriculture and the countryside like poetry. Wordsworth's 'Daffodils', included in this collection, is said by some to have done more for our collective appreciation of what our countryside can provide than any other piece of writing. This anthology contains many more examples of words mirroring the beauty of our soil and landscape.

As President of The Royal Agricultural College, it gives me great pleasure to contribute to this anthology and I hope it captures, for all its readers, some of the many facets and delights of Nature and – even more importantly, all that She provides for us and which, regrettably, is all too often taken for granted and abused. Poetry and harmony often go together – it is high time we worked more in harmony with Nature once again and recognized what is truly Sacred.

Charles

HRH the Prince of Wales
President of The Royal Agricultural College

Royal Agricultural College

Arvorum Cultus Pecorumque

The Royal Agricultural College's motto is a quote from Virgil's *Georgics* and translates as 'Caring for the Fields and the Beasts.'

INTRODUCTION

The stimulus for this collection came from chance comments and conversations at The Royal Agricultural College around the role that poetry has played in expressing the enjoyment and value that we get from our land, and the need for this appreciation, and the appreciation of poetry generally, to be more widely shared. It is in many ways very timely, as society realises that 'the land' provides not just food, but also manages our water and our environment, provides leisure and other services, and does so under ever increasing pressure from human demand and climate change.

The anthology includes poems both well known and less often seen, modern and from earlier times, cheerful and less so, but all hopefully accessible to those relatively new to poetry and all serving to underline the richness and diversity to be found in 'our common ground'. We hope it provides much enjoyment and 'food for thought'.

Professor Christopher Gaskell
The Principal, Royal Agricultural College

ACKNOWLEDGEMENTS

The editors gratefully acknowledge the generosity and assistance of:

- HRH the Prince of Wales, President of The Royal Agricultural College, for his support for this anthology;
- the College Principal, Professor Christopher Gaskell BVSc, PhD, DVR, MRCVS and Jonathan Taylor CBE for their original vision for the anthology, and their encouragement of the editors;
- Abigail Portus for her artistic input, and Cirencester College for facilitating this;
- those poets or their publishers, agents and executors who have generously allowed us to reproduce their poems without – or at a reduced – fee;
- Alex Murray at Silverdart Publishing for his assistance and patience;
- everyone who has kindly suggested poets and poems for inclusion in this anthology; and
- the poets whose works are no longer in copyright for their exploration of, and insights into, 'our common ground' over the centuries.

The Royal Agricultural College is particularly grateful to Handelsbanken for its sponsorship of the first edition of this anthology.

The editors apologise for any omissions or errors which may have crept in despite their diligence, and accept full responsibility for the same.

Although the editors have tried to contact all copyright holders before publication, this has not proved possible in every case. They will be pleased to hear from any such rights-holders. For a list of poets showing sources and acknowledgements, please see page 145.

CONTENTS

CONTENTS

On Farming

CYNDDYLAN ON A TRACTOR
by RS Thomas

Ronald Stuart Thomas, 1913-2000, is one of the best-known Welsh poets. He was ordained as an Anglican clergyman in 1936, spending his whole time working in rural parishes.

Ah, you should see Cynddylan on a tractor.
Gone the old look that yoked him to the soil,
He's a new man now, part of the machine,
His nerves of metal and his blood oil.
The clutch curses, but the gears obey
His least bidding, and lo, he's away
Out of the farmyard, scattering hens.
Riding to work now as a great man should,
He is the knight at arms breaking the fields'
Mirror of silence, emptying the wood
Of foxes and squirrels and bright jays.
The sun comes over the tall trees
Kindling all the hedges, but not for him
Who runs his engine on a different fuel.
And all the birds are singing, bills wide in vain,
As Cynddylan passes proudly up the lane.

FOLLOWER
by Seamus Heaney

Seamus Heaney, born 1933, grew up on his family's 50 acre farm in Northern Ireland. His father particularly loved cattle dealing. Much of Heaney's poetry is grounded in rural County Derry. He was awarded the Nobel Prize in Literature in 1995.

My father worked with a horse-plough,
His shoulders globed like a full sail strung
Between the shafts and the furrow.
The horse strained at his clicking tongue.

An expert. He would set the wing
And fit the bright steel-pointed sock.
The sod rolled over without breaking.
At the headrig, with a single pluck

Of reins, the sweating team turned round
And back into the land. His eye
Narrowed and angled at the ground,
Mapping the furrow exactly.

I stumbled in his hob-nailed wake,
Fell sometimes on the polished sod;
Sometimes he rode me on his back
Dipping and rising to his plod.

I wanted to grow up and plough,
To close one eye, stiffen my arm.
All I ever did was follow
In his broad shadow round the farm.

I was a nuisance, tripping, falling,
Yapping always. But today
It is my father who keeps stumbling
Behind me, and will not go away.

THISTLE
by Vona Groarke

Vona Groarke, born 1964, is an award-winning Irish poet.

> 'And love ties a woman's mind
> looser than with ropes of hay.'
> Andrew Marvell,
> *Ametas and Thestylis Making Hay Ropes*

It's hard to get away from hay these days,
what with the warm weather and the news
from home. Last year the price was high,
but this year they'll be giving it away.
The fields are stitched and cross-stitched
with its high-wire bales: the smell is such
I find I'm driving with all the windows down
past rows of unstooped and bare-chested men

which pass for a vision of the pastoral round here.
As I may have done to some different car
and another driver crossing our farmgate once
when July was in heat. My father paid fifty pence
to the two of us for a full day's work –
me to the weeding, my brother to his fork –
but the men had their serious labour. I was the only girl
in a field bristling with hands, a stray in the herd.

My brother worked with them from the middle out
and I picked the edges clean of thistles and ragwort.
I was for hedges, he for height,
already eyeing up the stacks he'd make of it
in the barn, thinking taller with each trailer
from the fields, until he was pressed against the rafters
and had to stoop as I did, row on row,
in my small, careful and remunerated way.

That meadow gave good hay year in, year out.
We'd use what was needed, sell what was not
and see it off on the back of another man's jeep
to farms with too little grass, too many weeds.
Long after my hands healed over the thistle barbs
and the summer was closeted in cardigans and scarves,
that hay was holding out awhile over those lean
weeks while the weather righted and the year filled in.

Until I found myself head-high to the heat of a day,
singing again to the frogs and the stiffening hay,
small words in a small tune to kill the hours
that skirted their rough talk and fine acres.
What we saved there was unpoisonous and sweet
and it came again as the same meadow, the same weeds,
the same hay I last made when I was twelve,
the same ragwort I discarded, that still thrives.

FETCHING COWS
by Norman MacCaig

Norman MacCaig, 1910-1996, was a prolific Scottish poet who wrote with economy and precision. Though born in Edinburgh he spent much of his time in a remote area of North-West Scotland. His pacifist views also meant that he spent time doing landwork during World War Two.

The black one, last as usual, swings her head
And coils a black tongue round a grass-tuft. I
Watch her soft weight come down, her split feet spread.

In front, the others swing and slouch; they roll
Their great Greek eyes and breathe out milky gusts
From muzzles black and shiny as wet coal.

The collie trots, bored, at my heels, then plops
Into the ditch. The sea makes a tired sound
That's almost stopping though it never stops.

A haycart squats prickeared against the sky.
Hay breath and milk breath. Far out in the West
The wrecked sun founders though its colours fly.

The collie's bored. There's nothing to control...
The black cow is two native carriers
Bringing its belly home, slung from a pole.

MUCK SPREADING
by Geoffrey K Nelson

Geoffrey Kenneth Nelson, born 1923, began his working life on a farm. Since then he has published a number of books on social history including To Be a Farmer's Boy which chronicles changes in farming in the first half of the 20th century.

A warm job on a winter's day
is carting muck from the midden
up in waggons that bump and sway
along the wrinkled, rut sodden,
track, from par yard to fog swathed
fields, where the horses' hot breath steams
upon the silent mornings wreathed
air. While weeping from the dreaming
trees the grey skies drop their sorrow
in good hope of a fair morrow,

Now in the fields they spread the spoil
rich, ripe and odorous across
broad acres of the sleeping soil,
for on the farm there is no loss.
For from autumns lavish spending,
nought wasted, earth recycles all.
Spring bloom and summer fruit sending
and golden harvests in the Fall.

All throughout the year each
dying brings new life. See
where white fungi flourish
on that dead decaying tree.

THE MANOR FARM
by Edward Thomas

Edward Thomas, 1878-1917, was killed in action aged just 39 in France in World War One and is often considered a war poet, though much of his poetry is rooted in the English countryside. He is also known as one of the 'Dymock poets', a literary group, some of whose members made their home near this Gloucestershire village.

The rock-like mud unfroze a little, and rills
Ran and sparkled down each side of the road
Under the catkins wagging in the hedge.
But earth would have her sleep out, spite of the sun;
Nor did I value that thin gliding beam
More than a pretty February thing
Till I came down to the old manor farm,
And church and yew-tree opposite, in age
Its equals and in size. The church and yew
And farmhouse slept in a Sunday silentness.
The air raised not a straw. The steep farm roof,
With tiles duskily glowing, entertained
The mid-day sun; and up and down the roof
White pigeons nestled. There was no sound but one.
Three cart horses were looking over a gate
Drowsily through their forelocks, swishing their tails
Against a fly, a solitary fly.
The winter's cheek flushed as if he had drained
Spring, summer, and autumn at a draught
And smiled quietly. But 'twas not winter -
Rather a season of bliss unchangeable,
Awakened from farm and church where it had lain
Safe under tile and latch for ages since
This England, Old already, was called Merry.

MILLET: THE GLEANERS
by Simon Armitage

Simon Armitage, born 1963, is a modern poet and writer who has won both popular and critical acclaim. His poem below makes reference to Millet's 1857 golden-hued painting of French agricultural labourers.

No one's twisting her arm but there it is,
locked backwards in a half-nelson, broken
like a shotgun. In hand, a spray of corn
spills out like a tail of peahen feathers.

The nearest is standing but bends also.
Like a forced branch or a trained limb, something
which has given, she curves, disarmed, a bow
without string hemmed in under the skyline.

The third shadows the first, and if the sunset
is a spotlight then she steals the finale
with a bow, not a curtsy. Past caring
she forgets the task, if it was picking
or planting, whether it was corn or barley.

Let me say this: we trip across the fields
like tourists; take flowers, tell huge stories –
lies, and think only of the poppies.
It could be midnight when the evening fades;

the hammock, the hats, the picnic basket,
the day like an apple not even bruised
but somehow bottled, the road in sight, the car
where we left it. It will right itself, that square
of flattened grass where we laid the blanket.

THE FIELD, TOMORROW
by George MacBeth

George Mann MacBeth, 1932-1992, was a Scottish poet and novelist.

I wanted the bare field out there to be mine.
Each day, at my typing, I saw the smooth line

Of the sycamores, breaking the sweep of the grass
To the farm and the river. I saw the sails pass

Far away, white and simple, where yachts moved at Thurne.
And I looked down, in pride, at my nearest stone urn.

From that urn to the sycamores, this was my land,
With the wide breadth of Norfolk stretched gold on each hand.

I had space, in my dream, and six acres to keep.
I had grass for my garden, and twenty new sheep.

It's all over. The field has been sold, to my friends,
And the dream of broad acres, all hope of it, ends.

At the auction I bid high, too high for my good,
And I'm glad that I missed it, at that price. I should

Have been forced into borrowing, bound to the shape
Of solicitor's ropes. But it still feels like rape

To see horses, brown horses, that other men own
(In my mind they seem galloping, sculptured like stone)

Out there in my bare field. I touch them, and weep,
And remember my dream, and the slow-moving sheep,

Their cold, lovely fleece, and their beautiful eyes,
And their mouths, low and cropping, surrounded by flies.

BURNING OFF
by Maureen Duffy

Maureeen Duffy, born 1933, is a contemporary British poet, playwright and novelist. Her work often incorporates elements from myth and history.

Already autumn stains
a branch here and there
singles out leaves to stopper
their narrow veins with drought
though August's barely out.

Yesterday the yellow combine
tanked through corn
a minotaur carving
its own labyrinth
an iron whopstraw[1].

A cropped bright stubble
five o'clocks the fields
with stiff gold shafts
one night, then flares
is barbequed black.

Small pointed skulls cremate
slim runners' bones
stripped of sinew crumble
where the smoke stopped them
in their secret track.

These yearly harrowings
libations some god demands
are old as husbandry.
Once it was the delicate seed
of lovers in field or wood.

1. Thresher

Now the ground trembles
under a metal stamp muting
the birds' alarm in the broken air.
At night the field is smeared black
under a drained moon.

Morning breaks
in a cold sweat of mist.
The motorway's a distant surf
I launch into. Returning
I drive through a still smutted sunset.

The junctions fall away
at summer's end.
That's where I turned off
in Spring when last year's seed
lay flecked with bonemeal in the ground.

Home again I walk
the unburnt stubble behind my house.
Tomorrow you fly back.
I should pour my heart's blood
out for luck. I do.

THE HARVEST OF THE MIND
by Michael Shepherd

Michael Shepherd, 1929-2010, went to Oxford before dropping out, later becoming an art critic and poet.

Consider for a while,
deeper mind as agriculture:

garnered seeds at rightful time –
deeds as seeds –
surrendered to the wisdom of the earth
which contains the wisdom
of all other elements:

surrendered to the faith in nature,
hope of harvest;

in the meantime, nought to do
but pray and praise and cultivate
that inner earth; care
for next year's seeding field;

repair the fences of discrimination; trim
the hedges, spinneys, copses,
where free nature of herself displays
so beautifully, that which is.

BREAD AND BUTTER LETTER
(to Philip and Barbara Rawson)
by Michael Hamburger

Michael Hamburger, 1924-2007, was born into a German family of Jewish descent in Berlin, emigrating with them to England in 1933. He settled in rural Suffolk and was a knowledgeable gardener and amateur horticulturalist, preserving rare varieties of apple tree by growing them from seed.

Bread is the fields of wheat
Where partridges creaked in flight,
Faint hum of daytime tractor,
The fidgeted drum of night;
Butter the mushroomed pastures,
Meadow and muddy patch,
Parched where the clumps and the mounds are,
Sodden in hollow and ditch.

And water: the shallow river
With willow, lily and rush,
Then the sudden pool, no wider,
Though deep as diver could wish.

These are not you nor yours
To keep or to give away:
This barn you did not build
Nor saved the roof from decay;
Yet its ruin's pattern grew fertile
When the skeleton pierced your gaze
To be more than thatched in thought
To leap alive from your eyes.

As from ridge and furrow we gather
The spirit behind the face
And lovers even must look for
Their love's true dwelling-place,
Praising the site of your tenure

I praise both mind and thing:
Their marriage, from which all beauty
And all creation spring.

May garden, orchard and meadow,
Cornfield, river and pool
Nourish your art and prove
As ever bountiful,
Lest the abstract cities wither
That primal intergrowth
Of outward form and inward,
Levelling all into death.

May all your bread be fields of wheat
And the dual pastures requite
With dual blessings your labour,
No daemon darken your site.

THE HOE SCRAPES EARTH
by Ivor Gurney

The evocation by Ivor Gurney, 1890-1937, of the beauty of the English rural landscape is in strong contrast to his war poetry. A member of the Gloucestershire Regiment, he was wounded and gassed in 1917 while serving at the front.

The hoe scrapes earth as fine in grain as sand,
I like the swirl of it and the swing in the hand
Of the lithe hoe so clever at craft and grace,
And the friendliness the clear freedom of the place.

And the green hairs of the wheat on the sandy brown
The draw of eyes toward the coloured town,
The lark ascending slow to a roof of cloud
That cries for the voice of poetry to cry aloud.

Our Countryside

ADLESTROP
by Edward Thomas

Adlestrop is a village in Gloucestershire. The poem describes a train journey which Edward Thomas, 1878-1917, took in 1914. The train made an unscheduled stop at Adlestrop station. He did not alight, but the halt made an impression leading to a poem that has immortalised the village throughout the English-speaking world.

Yes. I remember Adlestrop –
The name, because one afternoon
Of heat the express-train drew up there
Unwontedly. It was late June.

The steam hissed. Someone cleared his throat.
No one left and no one came
On the bare platform. What I saw
Was Adlestrop – only the name

And willows, willow-herb, and grass,
And meadowsweet, and haycocks dry,
No whit less still and lonely fair
Than the high cloudlets in the sky.

And for that minute a blackbird sang
Close by, and round him, mistier,
Farther and farther, all the birds
Of Oxfordshire and Gloucestershire.

THE BEEKEEPER
by Ann Williams

Ann Williams, born 1954, is a modern poet who married into a farming family in East Sussex. Agriculture is a subject close to her heart and her poetry.

At weekends, he pretended to hang his own skin
behind the kitchen door. No use with bees,
he'd tease and disappear. For years we'd lose
him then; on still summer days a shadow figure
magnified on the whitewashed wall was all we knew.

But as we grew, we learned more of his magic.
Followed unbidden the curls of acrid smoke
to watch, open-mouthed, as he calmed the fizzing bees
to a gentle hum, raising the domed roof of the lid.
Inching forward we hid and held our breath.

Years later, visiting him, only a short walk from death,
his ill-fitting paper-thin fingers holding mine,
I remember how he had looked back then, as
turning he held out a gloved hand covered with bees
for us to see something of the tenacity of love.

His hands danced in and out of shadow
in the dappled light, under the trees, working
an invisible alchemy of their own.

TO DAFFODILS
by Robert Herrick

Robert Herrick, 1591-1674, was influenced by classical poetry and wrote on pastoral themes dealing with English country life. Often, as in this poem, he reminds us that life is short and the world beautiful, and we must use the short time we have to make the most of it.

Fair Daffodils, we weep to see
You haste away so soon;
As yet the early-rising sun
Has not attain'd his noon.
Stay, stay,
Until the hasting day
Has run
But to the even-song;
And, having pray'd together, we
Will go with you along.

We have short time to stay, as you,
We have as short a spring;
As quick a growth to meet decay,
As you, or anything.
We die
As your hours do, and dry
Away,
Like to the summer's rain;
Or as the pearls of morning's dew,
Ne'er to be found again.

DAFFODILS
by William Wordsworth

This much-anthologised poem was voted fifth in a BBC poll of the nation's 100 most loved poems. It was inspired by the sight of daffodils while William Wordsworth, 1770-1850, was on a walk in the Lake District.

I wander'd lonely as a cloud
That floats on high o'er vales and hills,
When all at once I saw a crowd,

A host, of golden daffodils;
Beside the lake, beneath the trees,
Fluttering and dancing in the breeze.
Continuous as the stars that shine

And twinkle on the Milky Way,
They stretch'd in never-ending line

Along the margin of a bay:
Ten thousand saw I at a glance,
Tossing their heads in sprightly dance.
The waves beside them danced; but they

Out-did the sparkling waves in glee:
A poet could not but be gay,

In such a jocund company:
I gazed – and gazed – but little thought
What wealth the show to me had brought:
For oft, when on my couch I lie

In vacant or in pensive mood,
They flash upon that inward eye

Which is the bliss of solitude;
And then my heart with pleasure fills,
And dances with the daffodils.

FERN HILL
by Dylan Thomas

Although born in the town of Swansea, Dylan Thomas, 1914-1953, often made regular summer trips to his maternal aunts' Camarthenshire farms. The sharp contrast with town life inspired poems such as Fern Hill.

Now as I was young and easy under the apple boughs
About the lilting house and happy as the grass was green,
The night above the dingle starry,
Time let me hail and climb
Golden in the heydays of his eyes,
And honoured among wagons I was prince of the apple towns
And once below a time I lordly had the trees and leaves
Trail with daisies and barley
Down the rivers of the windfall light.

And as I was green and carefree, famous among the barns
About the happy yard and singing as the farm was home,
In the sun that is young once only,
Time let me play and be
Golden in the mercy of his means,
And green and golden I was huntsman and herdsman, the calves
Sang to my horn, the foxes on the hills barked clear and cold,
And the sabbath rang slowly
In the pebbles of the holy streams.

All the sun long it was running, it was lovely, the hay
Fields high as the house, the tunes from the chimneys, it was air
And playing, lovely and watery
And fire green as grass.
And nightly under the simple stars
As I rode to sleep the owls were bearing the farm away,
All the moon long I heard, blessed among stables, the nightjars
Flying with the ricks, and the horses
Flashing into the dark.

And then to awake, and the farm, like a wanderer white
With the dew, come back, the cock on his shoulder: it was all
Shining, it was Adam and maiden,
The sky gathered again
And the sun grew round that very day.
So it must have been after the birth of the simple light
In the first, spinning place, the spellbound horses walking warm
Out of the whinnying green stable
On to the fields of praise.

And honoured among foxes and pheasants by the gay house
Under the new made clouds and happy as the heart was long,
In the sun born over and over,
I ran my heedless ways,
My wishes raced through the house high hay
And nothing I cared, at my sky blue trades, that time allows
In all his tuneful turning so few and such morning songs
Before the children green and golden
Follow him out of grace.

Nothing I cared, in the lamb white days, that time would take me
Up to the swallow thronged loft by the shadow of my hand,
In the moon that is always rising,
Nor that riding to sleep
I should hear him fly with the high fields
And wake to the farm forever fled from the childless land.
Oh as I was young and easy in the mercy of his means,
Time held me green and dying
Though I sang in my chains like the sea.

MAGDALEN WALKS
by Oscar Wilde

Oscar Wilde, 1854-1900, gained the Berkeley Gold Medal for Greek at Trinity College, Dublin, in 1874 before proceeding to Oxford, where he obtained a scholarship to Magdalen College. He published his first collection of poetry in 1881.

The little white clouds are racing over the sky,
And the fields are strewn with the gold of the flower of March,
The daffodil breaks under foot, and the tasselled larch
Sways and swings as the thrush goes hurrying by.

A delicate odour is borne on the wings of the morning breeze,
The odour of deep wet grass, and of brown new-furrowed earth,
The birds are singing for joy of the Spring's glad birth,
Hopping from branch to branch on the rocking trees.

And all the woods are alive with the murmur and sound of Spring,
And the rose-bud breaks into pink on the climbing briar,
And the crocus-bed is a quivering moon of fire
Girdled round with the belt of an amethyst ring.

And the plane to the pine-tree is whispering some tale of love
Till it rustles with laughter and tosses its mantle of green,
And the gloom of the wych-elm's hollow is lit with the iris sheen
Of the burnished rainbow throat and the silver breast of a dove.

See! the lark starts up from his bed in the meadow there,
Breaking the gossamer threads and the nets of dew,
And flashing adown the river, a flame of blue!
The kingfisher flies like an arrow, and wounds the air.

WALKING
by Thomas Traherne

Thomas Traherne, 1636-1674, was one of the 17th century group of poets known as the 'metaphysical poets'. His poems often explore the glories of creation and the visionary innocence of childhood. In this respect he prefigures later poets such as Blake and Wordsworth.

To walk abroad is, not with eyes,
But thoughts, the fields to see and prize;
Else may the silent feet,
Like logs of wood,
Move up and down, and see no good
Nor joy nor glory meet.

Ev'n carts and wheels their place do change,
But cannot see, though very strange
The glory that is by;
Dead puppets may
Move in the bright and glorious day,
Yet not behold the sky.

And are not men than they more blind,
Who having eyes yet never find
The bliss in which they move;
Like statues dead
They up and down are carried
Yet never see nor love.

To walk is by a thought to go;
To move in spirit to and fro;
To mind the good we see;
To taste the sweet;
Observing all the things we meet
How choice and rich they be.

To note the beauty of the day,
And golden fields of corn survey;

Admire each pretty flow'r
With its sweet smell;
To praise their Maker, and to tell
The marks of his great pow'r.

To fly abroad like active bees,
Among the hedges and the trees,
To cull the dew that lies
On ev'ry blade,
From ev'ry blossom; till we lade
Our minds, as they their thighs.

Observe those rich and glorious things,
The rivers, meadows, woods, and springs,
The fructifying sun;
To note from far
The rising of each twinkling star
For us his race to run.

A little child these well perceives,
Who, tumbling in green grass and leaves,
May rich as kings be thought,
But there's a sight
Which perfect manhood may delight,
To which we shall be brought.

While in those pleasant paths we talk,
'Tis that tow'rds which at last we walk;
For we may by degrees
Wisely proceed
Pleasures of love and praise to heed,
From viewing herbs and trees.

ON EASTNOR KNOLL
by John Masefield

John Masefield, 1878-1967, was an English poet and writer, and Poet Laureate from 1930 until his death. He was born in Ledbury, and later moved to Oxford where he kept bees, goats and poultry. In the 1930s he moved to Pinbury Park near Sapperton, Cirencester.

Silent are the woods, and the dim green boughs are
Hushed in the twilight: yonder, in the path through
The apple orchard, is a tired plough-boy
Calling the cows home.

A bright white star blinks, the pale moon rounds, but
Still the red, lurid wreckage of the sunset
Smoulders in smoky fire, and burns on
The misty hill-tops.

Ghostly it grows, and darker, the burning
Fades into smoke, and now the gusty oaks are
A silent army of phantoms thronging
A land of shadows.

GOBLIN MARKET (extract)
by Christina Georgina Rossetti

Goblin Market, a verse fairy tale written by Christina Georgina Rossetti, 1830-1894, was published in 1862. It tells a wonderfully sensuous story that has inspired a myriad of interpretations. Here you can simply enjoy the evocation of the eponymous Goblins' abundant supply of fruit.

Morning and evening
Maids heard the goblins cry:
"Come buy our orchard fruits,
Come buy, come buy:
Apples and quinces,
Lemons and oranges,
Plump unpecked cherries-
Melons and raspberries,
Bloom-down-cheeked peaches,
Swart-headed mulberries,
Wild free-born cranberries,
Crab-apples, dewberries,
Pine-apples, blackberries,
Apricots, strawberries –
All ripe together
In summer weather –
Morns that pass by,
Fair eves that fly;
Come buy, come buy;
Our grapes fresh from the vine,
Pomegranates full and fine,
Dates and sharp bullaces,
Rare pears and greengages,
Damsons and bilberries,
Taste them and try:
Currants and gooseberries,
Bright-fire-like barberries,
Figs to fill your mouth,
Citrons from the South,
Sweet to tongue and sound to eye,
Come buy, come buy."

TINTERN ABBEY (extract)
by William Wordsworth

The full title of the following poem is Lines Composed a Few Miles above Tintern Abbey, on Revisiting the Banks of the Wye during a Tour, July 13 1798. It describes and encapsulates Wordsworth's almost pantheistic view of nature.

... And so I dare to hope,
Though changed, no doubt, from what I was when first
I came among these hills; when like a roe
I bounded o'er the mountains, by the sides
Of the deep rivers, and the lonely streams,
Wherever nature led: more like a man
Flying from something that he dreads, than one
Who sought the thing he loved. For nature then
(The coarser pleasures of my boyish days,
And their glad animal movements all gone by)
To me was all in all. – I cannot paint
What then I was. The sounding cataract
Haunted me like a passion: the tall rock,
The mountain, and the deep and gloomy wood,
Their colours and their forms, were then to me
An appetite; a feeling and a love,
That had no need of a remoter charm,
By thought supplied, nor any interest
Unborrowed from the eye. – That time is past,
And all its aching joys are now no more,
And all its dizzy raptures. Not for this
Faint I, nor mourn nor murmur, other gifts
Have followed; for such loss, I would believe,
Abundant recompence. For I have learned
To look on nature, not as in the hour
Of thoughtless youth; but hearing oftentimes
The still, sad music of humanity,
Nor harsh nor grating, though of ample power
To chasten and subdue. And I have felt
A presence that disturbs me with the joy

Of elevated thoughts; a sense sublime
Of something far more deeply interfused,
Whose dwelling is the light of setting suns,
And the round ocean and the living air,
And the blue sky, and in the mind of man;
A motion and a spirit, that impels
All thinking things, all objects of all thought,
And rolls through all things. Therefore am I still
A lover of the meadows and the woods,
And mountains; and of all that we behold
From this green earth; of all the mighty world
Of eye, and ear, – both what they half create,
And what perceive; well pleased to recognise
In nature and the language of the sense,
The anchor of my purest thoughts, the nurse,
The guide, the guardian of my heart, and soul
Of all my moral being.

LACHIN Y GAIR (extract)
by Lord Byron

Lord Byron, 1788-1824, though born in England, spent his formative childhood years in Scotland. The following poem suggests that the Scottish landscape made a deep impression on him. Loch na Garr (or Lochnagar) is a mountain close to the Royal estate of Balmoral in Aberdeenshire.

Away, ye gay landscapes, ye garden of roses!
In you let the minions of luxury rove;
Restore me the rocks, where the snow-flake reposes,
Though still they are sacred to freedom and love:
Yet, Caledonia, beloved are thy mountains,
Round their white summits though elements war;
Though cataracts foam 'stead of smooth-flowing fountains,
I sigh for the valley of dark Loch na Garr ...

... Years have roll'd on, Loch na Garr, since I left you,
Years must elapse ere I tread you again:
Nature of verdure and flow'rs has bereft you,
Yet still are you dearer than Albion's plain.
England! thy beauties are tame and domestic
To one who has roved o'er the mountains afar:
Oh for the crags that are wild and majestic!
The steep frowning glories of dark Loch na Garr!

IN TINTAGEL GRAVEYARD
by Brian Patten

Brian Patten, born 1946, first made his name in the 1960s as one of the 'Liverpool poets'. Of this poem Patten has written, "In an ancient cemetery overlooking the sea, I saw fresh flowers that had been placed on the grave of a boy who had drowned more than a century ago".

Who brought flowers to this grave?
I, said the wren.
I brought them as seeds and then
Watched them grow.

No, said the wind. That's not true.
I blew them across the moor and sea,
I blew them up to the grave's door.
They were a gift from me.

They came of their own accord,
Said the celandine.
I know best. They're brothers of mine.

I am Death's friend,
Said the crow. I ought to know.
I dropped them into the shadow of the leaning stone.
I brought the flowers.

No, said Love,
It was I who brought them,

With the help of the wren's wing,
With the help of the wind's breath,
With the help of the celandine and the crow.

It was I who brought them
For the living and the dead to share,
I was the force that put those flowers there.

SOIL
by Roger McGough

Roger McGough, born 1937, is another of the trio of 'Liverpool poets', the third being Adrian Henri. Their poetry is immediate and accessible, and often shot through with humour.

we've ignored eachother for a long time
and I'm strictly an indoor man
anytime to call would be the wrong time
I'll avoid you as long as I can

When I was a boy we were good friends
I made pies out of you when you were wet
And in childhood's remembered summer weather
We roughandtumbled together
We were very close

just you and me and the sun
the world a place for having fun
always so much to be done

But gradually I grew away from you
Of course you were still there
During my earliest sexcapades
When I roughandfumbled
Not very well after bedtime
But suddenly it was winter
And you seemed so cold and dirty
That I stayed indoors and acquired
A taste for girls and clean clothes

we found less and less to say
you were jealous so one day
I simply upped and moved away

I still called to see you on occasions
But we had little now in common

And my visits grew less frequent
Until finally
One coldbright April morning
A handful of you drummed
On my fathers waxworked coffin

at last it all made sense
there was no need for pretence
you said nothing in defence

And now recently
While travelling from town to town
Past where you live
I have become increasingly aware
Of you watching me out there.
Patient and unforgiving
Fidgeting with the trees.

we've avoided eachother for a long time
and I'm strictly a city man
anytime to call would be the wrong time
I'll avoid you as long as I can.

HOME THOUGHTS FROM ABROAD
by Robert Browning

Robert Browning, 1812-1889, spent many years abroad, especially in Italy, and his distance from home may well have inspired one of his – and British poetry's – best-known verses of the Victorian era.

Oh, to be in England
Now that April's there,
And whoever wakes in England
Sees, some morning, unaware,
That the lowest boughs and the brushwood sheaf
Round the elm-tree bole are in tiny leaf,
While the chaffinch sings on the orchard bough
In England – now!

And after April, when May follows,
And the whitethroat builds, and all the swallows!
Hark, where my blossomed pear-tree in the hedge
Leans to the field and scatters on the clover
Blossoms and dewdrops – at the bent spray's edge -
That's the wise thrush; he sings each song twice over,
Lest you should think he never could recapture
The first fine careless rapture!
And though the fields look rough with hoary dew,
All will be gay when noontide wakes anew
The buttercups, the little children's dower
– Far brighter than this gaudy melon-flower!

THE OLD VICARAGE, GRANTCHESTER (extract)
by Rupert Brooke

Like Edward Thomas, Rupert Brooke, 1887-1915, is associated with the 'Dymock poets'. The village of Grantchester to which this poem refers is in Cambridge where Brooke studied and lived for a time.

Ah God! to see the branches stir
Across the moon at Grantchester!
To smell the thrilling-sweet and rotten
Unforgettable, unforgotten
River-smell, and hear the breeze
Sobbing in the little trees.
Say, do the elm-clumps greatly stand
Still guardians of that holy land?
The chestnuts shade, in reverend dream,
The yet unacademic stream?
Is dawn a secret shy and cold
Anadyomene, silver-gold?
And sunset still a golden sea
From Haslingfield to Madingley?
And after, ere the night is born,
Do hares come out about the corn?
Oh, is the water sweet and cool,
Gentle and brown, above the pool?
And laughs the immortal river still
Under the mill, under the mill?
Say, is there Beauty yet to find?
And Certainty? and Quiet kind?
Deep meadows yet, for to forget
The lies, and truths, and pain? ...oh! yet
Stands the Church clock at ten to three?
And is there honey still for tea?

LITTLE GIDDING (extract from the Four Quartets)
by TS Eliot

American-born Thomas Stearns Eliot, 1888-1965, became a British citizen in 1927, the same year he converted to Anglicanism. Little Gidding is a village in Cambridgeshire that was once home to an Anglican community, and theological themes run through this poem.

Midwinter spring is its own season
Sempiternal though sodden towards sundown,
Suspended in time, between pole and tropic.
When the short day is brightest, with frost and fire,
The brief sun flames the ice, on pond and ditches,
In windless cold that is the heart's heat,
Reflecting in a watery mirror
A glare that is blindness in the early afternoon.
And glow more intense than blaze of branch, or brazier,
Stirs the dumb spirit: no wind, but pentecostal fire
In the dark time of the year. Between melting and freezing
The soul's sap quivers. There is no earth smell
Or smell of living thing. This is the spring time
But not in time's covenant. Now the hedgerow
Is blanched for an hour with transitory blossom
Of snow, a bloom more sudden
Than that of summer, neither budding nor fading,
Not in the scheme of generation.
Where is the summer, the unimaginable
Zero summer?

If you came this way,
Taking the route you would be likely to take
From the place you would be likely to come from,
If you came this way in may time, you would find the hedges
White again, in May, with voluptuary sweetness.
It would be the same at the end of the journey,
If you came at night like a broken king,
If you came by day not knowing what you came for,
It would be the same, when you leave the rough road

And turn behind the pig-sty to the dull facade
And the tombstone. And what you thought you came for
Is only a shell, a husk of meaning
From which the purpose breaks only when it is fulfilled
If at all. Either you had no purpose
Or the purpose is beyond the end you figured
And is altered in fulfilment. There are other places
Which also are the world's end, some at the sea jaws,
Or over a dark lake, in a desert or a city –
But this is the nearest, in place and time,
Now and in England.

PIED BEAUTY
by Gerard Manley Hopkins

Gerard Manley Hopkins, 1844-1889, was both a poet and Jesuit priest, and he often felt that the two callings were in conflict. As a result most of his poems were only published after his death. Many of them display a love of nature, an appreciation of the uniqueness of things and how they each manifest divinity. Both the imagery and rhythm of his poems is often striking.

Glory be to God for dappled things –
For skies of couple-colour as a brinded cow;
For rose-moles all in stipple upon trout that swim;
Fresh-firecoal chestnut-falls; finches' wings;
Landscape plotted and pieced – fold, fallow, and plough;
And áll trádes, their gear and tackle and trim.
All things counter, original, spare, strange;
Whatever is fickle, freckled (who knows how?)
With swift, slow; sweet, sour; adazzle, dim;
He fathers-forth whose beauty is past change: Praise Him.

BLACKBERRY-PICKING
by Seamus Heaney

This is another of Seamus Heaney's poems capturing the intensity of a childhood spent in rural Ireland.

Late August, given heavy rain and sun
for a full week, the blackberries would ripen.
At first, just one, a glossy purple clot
among others, red, green, hard as a knot.
You ate that first one and its flesh was sweet
like thickened wine: summer's blood was in it
leaving stains upon the tongue and lust for
picking. Then red ones inked up and that hunger
sent us out with milk-cans, pea-tins, jam-pots
where briars scratched and wet grass bleached our boots.
Round hayfields, cornfields and potato-drills
we trekked and picked until the cans were full,
until the tinkling bottom had been covered
with green ones, and on top big dark blobs burned
like a plate of eyes. Our hands were peppered
with thorn pricks, our palms sticky as Bluebeard's.
We hoarded the fresh berries in the byre.
But when the bath was filled we found a fur,
A rat-grey fungus, glutting on our cache.
The juice was stinking too. Once off the bush
the fruit fermented, the sweet flesh would turn sour.
I always felt like crying. It wasn't fair
that all the lovely canfuls smelt of rot.
Each year I hoped they'd keep, knew they would not.

ELEGY WRITTEN IN A COUNTRY CHURCHYARD (extract)
by Thomas Gray

'Elegy' was a great success when published in 1751, and continues to be the best-known work by Thomas Gray, 1716-1771. The poem is a meditation on mortality but is also deeply rooted in the English countryside.

The Curfew tolls the knell of parting day,
The lowing herd wind slowly o'er the lea,
The plowman homeward plods his weary way,
And leaves the world to darkness and to me.

Now fades the glimmering landscape on the sight,
And all the air a solemn stillness holds,
Save where the beetle wheels his droning flight,
And drowsy tinklings lull the distant folds;

Save that from yonder ivy-mantled tow'r
The moping owl does to the moon complain
Of such as, wand'ring near her secret bow'r,
Molest her ancient solitary reign.

Beneath those rugged elms, that yew-tree's shade,
Where heaves the turf in many a mould'ring heap,
Each in his narrow cell for ever laid,
The rude Forefathers of the hamlet sleep.

The breezy call of incense-breathing Morn,
The swallow twitt'ring from the straw-built shed,
The cock's shrill clarion, or the echoing horn,
No more shall rouse them from their lowly bed.

For them no more the blazing hearth shall burn,
Or busy housewife ply her evening care:
No children run to lisp their sire's return,
Or climb his knees the envied kiss to share.

Oft did the harvest to their sickle yield,
Their furrow oft the stubborn glebe has broke:
How jocund did they drive their team afield!
How bow'd the woods beneath their sturdy stroke!

Let not Ambition mock their useful toil,
Their homely joys, and destiny obscure;
Nor Grandeur hear with a disdainful smile
The short and simple annals of the poor.

The boast of heraldry, the pomp of pow'r,
And all that beauty, all that wealth e'er gave,
Awaits alike th' inevitable hour:
The paths of glory lead but to the grave.

I SAW A JOLLY HUNTER
by Charles Causley

Charles Causley, 1917-2003, was a Cornish poet and writer. Much of his work appeals equally to adults and to children.

I saw a jolly hunter
With a jolly gun
Walking in the country
In the jolly sun.

In the jolly meadow
Sat a jolly hare.
Saw the jolly hunter.
Took jolly care.

Hunter jolly eager-
Sight of jolly prey.
Forgot gun pointing
Wrong jolly way.

Jolly hunter jolly head
Over heels gone.
Jolly old safety catch
Not jolly on.

Bang went the jolly gun.
Hunter jolly dead.
Jolly hare got clean away.
Jolly good, I said.

THE OLD SQUIRE
by Wilfred Scawen Blunt

Wilfred Scawen Blunt, 1840-1922, was a poet, diplomat and traveller. He inherited the family's 4,000 acre estate, and he and his wife began collecting some of Egypt's finest Arabian horses. A number of them were shipped back to England, and the Crabbet Park Stud became an important Arabian breeding operation in England.

I like the hunting of the hare
Better than that of the fox;
I like the joyous morning air,
And the crowing of the cocks.

I like the calm of the early fields,
The ducks asleep by the lake,
The quiet hour which Nature yields
Before mankind is awake.

I like the pheasants and feeding things
Of the unsuspicious morn;
I like the flap of the wood-pigeon's wings
As she rises from the corn.

I like the blackbird's shriek, and his rush
From the turnips as I pass by,
And the partridge hiding her head in a bush,
For her young ones cannot fly.

I like these things, and I like to ride,
When all the world is in bed,
To the top of the hill where the sky grows wide,
And where the sun grows red.

The beagles at my horse heels trot
In silence after me;
There's Ruby, Roger, Diamond, Dot,
Old Slut and Margery, –

A score of names well used, and dear,
The names my childhood knew;
The horn, with which I rouse their cheer,
Is the horn my father blew.

I like the hunting of the hare
Better than that of the fox;
The new world still is all less fair
Than the old world it mocks.

I covet not a wider range
Than these dear manors give;
I take my pleasures without change,
And as I lived I live.

I leave my neighbors to their thought;
My choice it is, and pride,
On my own lands to find my sport,
In my own fields to ride.

The hare herself no better loves
The field where she was bred,
Than I the habit of these groves,
My own inherited.

I know my quarries every one,
The meuse where she sits low;
The road she chose to-day was run
A hundred years ago.

The lags, the gills, the forest ways,
The hedgerows one and all,
These are the kingdoms of my chase,
And bounded by my wall;

Nor has the world a better thing,
Though one should search it round,

Than thus to live one's own sole king,
Upon one's own sole ground.

I like the hunting of the hare;
It brings me, day by day,
The memory of old days as fair,
With dead men passed away.

To these, as homeward still I ply
And pass the churchyard gate,
Where all are laid as I must lie,
I stop and raise my hat.

I like the hunting of the hare;
New sports I hold in scorn.
I like to be as my fathers were,
In the days e'er I was born.

FOREFATHERS
by Edmund Blunden

Edmund Blunden, 1896-1974, spent his childhood in a typical 19th century working village in the Kent countryside. Though known too for his war poetry, the poems that reveal a deep love for the English countryside are often considered his best.

Here they went with smock and crook,
Toiled in the sun, lolled in the shade,
Here they mudded out the brook
And here their hatchet cleared the glade:
Harvest-supper woke their wit,
Huntsmen's moon their wooings lit.

From this church they led their brides,
From this church themselves were led
Shoulder-high; on these waysides
Sat to take their beer and bread.
Names are gone – what men they were
These their cottages declare.

Names are vanished, save the few
In the old brown Bible scrawled;
These were men of pith and thew,
Whom the city never called;
Scarce could read or hold a quill,
Built the barn, the forge, the mill.

On the green they watched their sons
Playing till too dark to see,
As their fathers watched them once,
As my father once watched me;
While the bat and beetle flew
On the warm air webbed with dew.

Unrecorded, unrenowned,
Men from whom my ways begin,

Here I know you by your ground
But I know you not within –
There is silence, there survives
Not a moment of your lives.

Like the bee that now is blown
Honey-heavy on my hand,
From his toppling tansy-throne
In the green tempestuous land –
I'm in clover now, nor know
Who made honey long ago.

NOW SLEEPS THE CRIMSON PETAL
by Alfred, Lord Tennyson

Alfred, Lord Tennyson, 1809-1892, was Poet Laureate through much of Queen Victoria's reign, and remains the defining poet of that age. His style is often referred to as 'lyrical', and the poem that follows has been set to music on several occasions.

Now sleeps the crimson petal, now the white;
Nor waves the cypress in the palace walk;
Nor winks the gold fin in the porphyry font;
The firefly wakens, waken thou with me.

Now droops the milk-white peacock like a ghost,
And like a ghost she glimmers on to me.

Now lies the Earth all Danae to the stars,
And all thy heart lies open unto me.

Now slides the silent meteor on, and leaves
A shining furrow, as thy thoughts, in me.

Now folds the lily all her sweetness up,
And slips into the bosom of the lake.
So fold thyself, my dearest, thou, and slip
Into my bosom and be lost in me.

THE ROLLING ENGLISH ROAD
by GK Chesterton

Gilbert Keith Chesterton, 1874-1936, was a prolific writer and today is probably best known for his Father Brown detective stories. The poem that follows skilfully combines rhyme, rhythm and alliteration to conjure up the idea of 'the rolling English road'.

Before the Roman came to Rye or out to Severn strode,
The rolling English drunkard made the rolling English road.
A reeling road, a rolling road, that rambles round the shire,
And after him the parson ran, the sexton and the squire;
A merry road, a mazy road, and such as we did tread
The night we went to Birmingham by way of Beachy Head.

I knew no harm of Bonaparte and plenty of the Squire,
And for to fight the Frenchman I did not much desire;
But I did bash their baggonets because they came arrayed
To straighten out the crooked road an English drunkard made,
Where you and I went down the lane with ale-mugs in our hands,
The night we went to Glastonbury by way of Goodwin Sands.

His sins they were forgiven him; or why do flowers run
Behind him; and the hedges all strengthening in the sun?
The wild thing went from left to right and knew not which was which,
But the wild rose was above him when they found him in the ditch.
God pardon us, nor harden us; we did not see so clear
The night we went to Bannockburn by way of Brighton Pier.

My friends, we will not go again or ape an ancient rage,
Or stretch the folly of our youth to be the shame of age,
But walk with clearer eyes and ears this path that wandereth,
And see undrugged in evening light the decent inn of death;
For there is good news yet to hear and fine things to be seen,
Before we go to Paradise by way of Kensal Green.

LEISURE
by William Henry Davies

William Henry Davies, 1871-1940, spent much of his life as a tramp in both England and the United States, and his simple, earthy poetry is largely on the subject of nature or life on the road. Leisure is his best known poem.

What is this life if, full of care,
We have no time to stand and stare.

No time to stand beneath the boughs
And stare as long as sheep or cows.

No time to see, when woods we pass,
Where squirrels hide their nuts in grass.

No time to see, in broad daylight,
Streams full of stars, like skies at night.

No time to turn at Beauty's glance,
And watch her feet, how they can dance.

No time to wait till her mouth can
Enrich that smile her eyes began.

A poor life this is if, full of care,
We have no time to stand and stare.

INTO MY HEART AN AIR THAT KILLS
by AE Housman

Alfred Edward Housman, 1859-1936, is best known for his cycle of poems called The Shropshire Lad, from which the following is taken. The poems are set in an idealised pastoral Shropshire, 'the land of lost content', whose hills he could see from near his childhood home in Worcestershire.

Into my heart an air that kills
From yon far country blows:
What are those blue remembered hills,
What spires, what farms are those?

That is the land of lost content,
I see it shining plain,
The happy highways where I went
And cannot come again.

THISTLES
by Ted Hughes

Ted Hughes, 1930-1998, was one of the 20th century's greatest poets. He was Poet Laureate from 1984 until his death. Raised among Yorkshire farms, he was also a keen countryman and hunter which may partly explain his unsentimental view of the natural world.

Against the rubber tongues of cows and the hoeing hands of men
Thistles spike the summer air
And crackle open under a blue-black pressure.

Every one a revengeful burst
Of resurrection, a grasped fistful
Of splintered weapons and Icelandic frost thrust up

From the underground stain of a decayed Viking.
They are like pale hair and the gutturals of dialects.
Every one manages a plume of blood.

Then they grow grey like men.
Mown down, it is a feud. Their sons appear
Stiff with weapons, fighting back over the same ground.

A MIDSUMMER NIGHT'S DREAM (extract from Act II, scene i)
by William Shakespeare

'A Midsummer Night's Dream', the well-known play by William Shakespeare, 1564-1616, is meant to take place in a wood near Athens, though the wildflowers so poetically described evoke the English countryside at least as much as the Greek.

[Oberon]
I know a bank where the wild thyme blows,
Where oxlips and the nodding violet grows,
Quite over-canopied with luscious woodbine,
With sweet musk-roses and with eglantine:
There sleeps Titania sometime of the night,
Lull'd in these flowers with dances and delight;
And there the snake throws her enamell'd skin,
Weed wide enough to wrap a fairy in...

THE GARDEN
by Andrew Marvell

Like Traherne, Andrew Marvell, 1621-1678, was a 'metaphysical poet' but is much more widely known than the former. This poem is a pastoral that reflects on a garden in a way that evokes the lost Garden of Eden.

How vainly men themselves amaze
To win the palm, the oak, or bays;
And their uncessant labors see
Crowned from some single herb or tree,
Whose short and narrow-vergèd shade
Does prudently their toils upbraid;
While all the flowers and trees do close
To weave the garlands of repose.

Fair Quiet, have I found thee here,
And Innocence, thy sister dear!
Mistaken long, I sought you then
In busy companies of men:
Your sacred plants, if here below,
Only among the plants will grow;
Society is all but rude,
To this delicious solitude.

No white nor red was ever seen
So amorous as this lovely green;
Fond lovers, cruel as their flame,
Cut in these trees their mistress' name.
Little, alas, they know or heed,
How far these beauties hers exceed!
Fair trees! wheresoe'er your barks I wound
No name shall but your own be found.

When we have run our passion's heat,
Love hither makes his best retreat:
The gods who mortal beauty chase,
Still in a tree did end their race.

Apollo hunted Daphne so,
Only that she might laurel grow,
And Pan did after Syrinx speed,
Not as a nymph, but for a reed.

What wondrous life is this I lead!
Ripe apples drop about my head;
The luscious clusters of the vine
Upon my mouth do crush their wine;
The nectarine and curious peach
Into my hands themselves do reach;
Stumbling on melons as I pass,
Insnared with flowers, I fall on grass.

Meanwhile the mind, from pleasure less,
Withdraws into its happiness:
The mind, that ocean where each kind
Does straight its own resemblance find;
Yet it creates, transcending these,
Far other worlds, and other seas;
Annihilating all that's made
To a green thought in a green shade.

Here at the fountain's sliding foot,
Or at some fruit-tree's mossy root,
Casting the body's vest aside,
My soul into the boughs does glide:
There like a bird it sits and sings,
Then whets and combs its silver wings;
And, till prepared for longer flight,
Waves in its plumes the various light.

Such was that happy garden-state,
While man there walked without a mate:
After a place so pure and sweet,
What other help could yet be meet!
But 'twas beyond a mortal's share
To wander solitary there:

Two paradises 'twere in one
To live in Paradise alone.

How well the skillful gard'ner drew
Of flowers and herbs this dial new;
Where from above the milder sun
Does through a fragrant zodiac run;
And, as it works, th' industrious bee
Computes its time as well as we.
How could such sweet and wholesome hours
Be reckoned but with herbs and flowers!

BEACHY HEAD (extract)
by Charlotte Smith

Charlotte Smith, 1749-1806, was an English Romantic poet and novelist. She was admired by Wordsworth, Coleridge and others although she was largely neglected and forgotten later on. However, the importance of her work is again being recognised, and it is not difficult to see parallels with Wordsworth's Tintern Abbey, also in this section.

An early worshipper at Nature's shrine;
I loved her rudest scenes – warrens, and heaths,
And yellow commons, and birch-shaded hollows,
And hedge rows, bordering unfrequented lanes
Bowered with wild roses, and the clasping woodbine
Where purple tassels of the tangling vetch
With bittersweet, and bryony inweave,
And the dew fills the silver bindweed's cups -
I loved to trace the brooks whose humid banks
Nourish the harebell, and the freckled pagil;
And stroll among o'ershadowing woods of beech,

Lending in summer, from the heats of noon
A whispering shade; while haply there reclines
Some pensive lover of uncultur'd flowers,
Who, from the tumps with bright green mosses clad,
Plucks the wood sorrel, with its light thin leaves,
Heart-shaped, and triply folded; and its root
Creeping like beaded coral; or who there
Gathers, the copse's pride, anemones,
With rays like golden studs on ivory laid
Most delicate: but touch'd with purple clouds,
Fit crown for April's fair but changeful brow.

Ah! hills so early loved! in fancy still
I breathe your pure keen air; and still behold
Those widely spreading views, mocking alike
The poet and the painter's utmost art.

WINDSOR FOREST (extract)
by Alexander Pope

Alexander Pope, 1688-1744, was a friend of the 1st Earl of Bathurst, whose family seat is Cirencester Park. Pope visited over a period of 30 years and advised his patron on the layout of the estate. 'Pope's Seat', a small rusticated stone pavilion in the parkland to the west of Cirencester House, can still be visited today.

The groves of Eden, vanish'd now so long,
Live in description, and look green in song:
These, were my breast inspir'd with equal flame,
Like them in beauty, should be like in fame.
Here hills and vales, the woodland and the plain,
Here earth and water, seem to strive again;
Not Chaos like together crush'd and bruis'd,
But as the world, harmoniously confus'd:
Where order in variety we see,
And where, tho' all things differ, all agree.
Here waving groves a chequer'd scene display,
And part admit, and part exclude the day;
As some coy nymph her lover's warm address
Nor quite indulges, nor can quite repress.
There, interspers'd in lawns and opening glades,
Thin trees arise that shun each other's shades.
Here in full light the russet plains extend;
There wrapt in clouds the blueish hills ascend.
Ev'n the wild heath displays her purple dyes,
And 'midst the desart fruitful fields arise,
That crown'd with tufted trees and springing corn,
Like verdant isles the sable waste adorn.
Let India boast her plants, nor envy we
The weeping amber or the balmy tree,
While by our oaks the precious loads are born,
And realms commanded which those trees adorn.
Not proud Olympus yields a nobler sight,
Tho' Gods assembled grace his tow'ring height,
Than what more humble mountains offer here,

Where, in their blessings, all those Gods appear.
See Pan with flocks, with fruits Pomona crown'd,
Here blushing Flora paints th' enamel'd ground,
Here Ceres' gifts in waving prospect stand,
And nodding tempt the joyful reaper's hand...

BUT THE TIMES, THEY MAY BE A-CHANGING
by Perkin Warrant

Perkin Warrant is a pseudonym of the English actor and writer Justin Edwards, born 1972. This is from 'The Odd Half Hour' on BBC's Radio 4.

I'm a potter by trade and I throw my clay
On my wheel and I fashion it all the long day
For in this old village dwelt stout rural folk
And the fields they were tilled by the plough and the yoke

But then from the city came bankers in droves
They converted our barns into fine weekend homes
They rag-rolled and refitted our tumbledown sheds
And sold them all off as apartments instead

Now the old village smithy will shoe no more mares
As his forge is now owned by some millionaire
Where once there were miners there's now web designers
The only cooper you'll find is the Pricewaterhouse kind

But I wasn't bothered to see the country folk go
Even though we had hedge funds instead of hedgerow
These new folk were rich, they had rural ambition
And I was the man to sell them tradition

For I flogged them my plates and I hawked them my pots
The fools thought them rustic, I knew they were crocks
The saucers were chipped, there were holes in the cups
But I said, "They're organic", and they lapped them up

Then comes the recession, they were skint in a week
They've got no pot to pee in, and mine would just leak
So I've lost my income now they've got no wedge
They've had to dig up their decking and grow their own veg

So the market's fallen out of my pottery fiddle
And I'm poor once again in my rustic old idyll

No money to burn since I can't fleece the toffs
We'll move to the city until they bog off

Seasons of the Year

WHILE YET WE WAIT FOR SPRING, AND FROM THE DRY
by Robert Bridges

Robert Bridges, 1844-1930, was Poet Laureate from 1913 until 1930. After illness forced him to retire from medical practice in 1882, he settled in rural Berkshire and Oxfordshire and devoted himself to writing poetry.

While yet we wait for spring, and from the dry
And blackening east that so embitters March,
Well-housed must watch grey fields and meadows parch,
And driven dust and withering snowflake fly;
Already in glimpses of the tarnish'd sky
The sun is warm and beckons to the larch,
And where the covert hazels interarch
Their tassell'd twigs, fair beds of primrose lie.
Beneath the crisp and wintry carpet hid
A million buds but stay their blossoming;
And trustful birds have built their nests amid
The shuddering boughs, and only wait to sing
Till one soft shower from the south shall bid,
And hither tempt the pilgrim steps of spring.

RETURN OF SPRING (extract from In Memoriam)
by Alfred, Lord Tennyson

This short poem is part of a much longer cycle of poems written following the unexpected death of Lord Tennyson's closest friend and confidante Arthur Henry Hallam, aged just 22.

Now fades the last long streak of snow,
Now burgeons every maze of quick
About the flowering squares, and thick
By ashen roots the violets blow.

Now rings the woodland loud and long,
The distance takes a lovelier hue,
And drown'd in yonder living blue
The lark becomes a sightless song.

Now dance the lights on lawn and lea,
The flocks are whiter down the vale,
And milkier every milky sail
On winding stream or distant sea;

Where now the seamew[2] pipes, or dives
In yonder greening gleam, and fly
The happy birds, that change their sky
To build and brood; that live their lives

From land to land; and in my breast
Spring wakens too; and my regret
Becomes an April violet,
And buds and blossoms like the rest.

2. Common Gull

AUGUST (extract from The Earthly Paradise)
by William Morris

William Morris, 1834-1896, was an English textile designer, artist, writer, and socialist associated with the Pre-Raphaelite Brotherhood and the English Arts and Crafts Movement

Across the gap made by our English hinds
Amidst the Roman's handiwork, behold
Far off the long-roofed church the shepherd binds
The withy round the hurdles of his fold
Down the foss the riverbed of old,
That through the long lapse of time has grown to be
The little grassy valley that you see.

Rest here awhile, not yet the eve is still,
The bees are wandering yet, and you may hear,
The barley mowers on the trenched hill,
The sheep-bells, and restless changing weir
All little sounds made musical and clear
Beneath the sky that burning August gives,
While yet the thought of glorious Summer lives.

THE SUMMER SUN SHONE ROUND ME
by Robert Louis Stevenson

Robert Louis Stevenson, 1850-1954, was a Scottish poet, novelist and essayist. He is best known for the novels Treasure Island, Kidnapped, and The Strange Case of Dr Jekyll and Mr Hyde.

The summer sun shone round me,
The folded valley lay
In a stream of sun and odour,
That sultry summer day.

The tall trees stood in the sunlight
As still as still could be,
But the deep grass sighed and rustled
And bowed and beckoned me.

The deep grass moved and whispered
And bowed and brushed my face.
It whispered in the sunshine:
"The winter comes apace."

DIGGING
by Edward Thomas

Here Edward Thomas, 1878-1917, uses the sense of smell to evoke the autumn and its elements of decay and regeneration.

Today I think
Only with scents, – scents dead leaves yield,
And bracken, and wild carrot's seed,
And the square mustard field;

Odours that rise
When the spade wounds the root of tree,
Rose, currant, raspberry, or goutweed,
Rhubarb or celery;

The smoke's smell, too
Flowing from where a bonfire burns
The dead, the waste, the dangerous,
And all to sweetness turns.

It is enough
To smell, to crumble the dark earth,
While the robin sings over again
Sad songs of Autumn mirth.

TO AUTUMN
by John Keats

In a letter written in September, 1819, John Keats, 1795-1821, says, "How beautiful the season is now – How fine the air. A temperate sharpness about it [...] I never lik'd stubble fields so much as now [...] Somehow a stubble plain looks warm – in the same way that some pictures look warm – this struck me so much in my sunday's walk that I composed upon it." What he composed was the ode below, often considered to be one of the finest poems in the English language.

Season of mists and mellow fruitfulness!
Close bosom-friend of the maturing sun;
Conspiring with him how to load and bless
With fruit the vines that round the thatch-eaves run;
To bend with apples the mossed cottage-trees,
And fill all fruit with ripeness to the core;
To swell the gourd, and plump the hazel shells
With a sweet kernel; to set budding more,
And still more, later flowers for the bees,
Until they think warm days will never cease,
For Summer has o'erbrimmed their clammy cells.

Who hath not seen thee oft amid thy store?
Sometimes whoever seeks abroad may find
Thee sitting careless on a granary floor,
Thy hair soft-lifted by the winnowing wind;
Or on a half-reaped furrow sound asleep,
Drowsed with the fume of poppies, while thy hook
Spares the next swath and all its twined flowers;
And sometimes like a gleaner thou dost keep
Steady thy laden head across a brook;
Or by a cider-press, with patient look,
Thou watchest the last oozings, hours by hours.

Where are the songs of Spring? Ay, where are they?
Think not of them, thou hast thy music too, –
While barred clouds bloom the soft-dying day

And touch the stubble-plains with rosy hue;
Then in a wailful choir the small gnats mourn
Among the river sallows, borne aloft
Or sinking as the light wind lives or dies;
And full-grown lambs loud bleat from hilly bourn;
Hedge-crickets sing, and now with treble soft
The redbreast whistles from a garden-croft;
And gathering swallows twitter in the skies.

WINTER (extract from The Land)
by Vita Sackville-West

Vita Sackville-West, 1892-1962, was an English author and poet, but she is perhaps best known today for the creation of Sissinghurst Garden in Kent, now owned by the National Trust.

I sing the cycle of my country's year,
I sing the tillage, and the reaping sing,
Classic monotony, that modes and wars
Leave undisturbed, unbettered, for their best
Was born immediate, of expediency.
The sickle sought no art; the axe, the share
Draped no superfluous beauty round their steel;
The scythe desired no music for her stroke,
Her stroke sufficed in music, as her blade
Laid low the swathes; the scythesmen swept, nor cared
What crop had ripened, whether oats in Greece
Or oats in Kent; the shepherd on the ridge
Like his Boeotian[3] forebear kept his flocks,
And still their outlines on our tenderer sky
Simple and classic rear their grave design
As once at Thebes, as once in Lombardy.

I sing once more
The mild continuous epic of the soil,
Haysel[4] and harvest, tilth and husbandry;
I tell of marl and dung, and of the means
That break the unkindly spirit of the clay;
I tell the things I know, the things I knew
Before I knew them, immemorially...

The country habit has me by the heart,
For he's bewitched forever who has seen,
Not with his eyes but with his vision, Spring

3. A region of Ancient Greece.
4. Haymaking season.

Flow down the woods and stipple leaves with sun,
As each man knows the life that fits him best,
The shape it makes in his soul, the tune, the tone,
And after ranging on a tentative flight
Stoops like the merlin to the constant lure.
The country habit has me by the heart.
I never hear the sheep bells in the fold,
Nor see the ungainly heron rise and flap
Over the marsh, nor hear the asprous corn
Clash, as the reapers set the sheaves in shocks
(That like a tented army dream away
The night beneath the moon in silver fields),
Nor watch the stubborn team of horse and man
Graven upon the skyline, nor regain
The sign posts on the roads towards my home
Bearing familiar names without a strong
Leaping of recognition; only here
Lies peace after uneasy truancy;
Here meet and marry many harmonies,
– All harmonies being ultimately one, –
Small mirroring majestic; for as earth
Rolls on her journey, so her little fields
Ripen or sleep, and the necessities
Of seasons match the planetary law.

In and Near the Cotswolds

SOLITUDE
by Arthur Noble

Arthur Noble taught for 26 years (1934-1960) at the Royal Agricultural College, where he was Head of the Estate Management Department. Affectionately known to generations of students as 'Uncle Arthur', Noble wrote a number of poems about the College and the Cotswolds. This poem was written deep in Cirencester Park.

I settle down on the bole of a beech
Laid low by the last year's storms,
Alone, on the edge of a woodland ride,
Midst nature in one of its forms.
With bronchial lungs and aging legs,
At an age near seventy seven,
I have strolled a mile from the tarmac road
For one more glimpse of Heaven.
The rustle of leaves in the standing beech
I catch through my hearing-aid,
And feel the sun that comes flickering through
The arch of a vernal glade.
Not a soul in sight, but bird-made sounds
Prove presence of living things
In this spot remote from the rat race life,
With the peace that solitude brings.
As I rest, I think that this must have been
The peace that our Saviour sought,
When taking himself to that lonely place,
Where the Devil's wiles he fought.
The fact that He won that battle then
And kept the Devil at bay
May well be the reason I can sit
And breathe in this stillness to-day.

TEWKESBURY ROAD
by John Masefield

There is evidence in the Royal Agricultural College Archive that John Masefield, 1878-1967, gave a poetry reading at the College in the 1930s, while Poet Laureate.

It is good to be out on the road, and going one knows not where,
Going through meadow and village, one knows not whither or why;
Through the grey light drift of the dust, in the keen cool rush of the air,
Under the flying white clouds, and the broad blue lift of the sky.

And to halt at the chattering brook, in a tall green fern at the brink
Where the harebell grows, and the gorse, and the foxgloves purple and white;
Where the shifty-eyed delicate deer troop down to the brook to drink
When the stars are mellow and large at the coming on of the night.

O, to feel the beat of the rain, and the homely smell of the earth,
Is a tune for the blood to jig to, and joy past power of words;
And the blessed green comely meadows are all a-ripple with mirth
At the noise of the lambs at play and the dear wild cry of the birds.

COTSWOLD LOVE
by John Drinkwater

John Drinkwater, 1882-1937, was an English poet and dramatist. Like Brooke and Edward Thomas he was one of the 'Dymock poets' and shared their profound appreciation of the English countryside.

Blue skies are over Cotswold
And April snows go by,
The lasses turn their ribbons
For April's in the sky,
And April is the season
When Sabbath girls are dressed,
From Rodboro' to Campden,
In all their silken best.

An ankle is a marvel
When first the buds are brown,
And not a lass but knows it
From Stow to Gloucester town.
And not a girl goes walking
Along the Cotswold lanes
But knows men's eyes in April
Are quicker than their brains.

It's little that it matters,
So long as you're alive,
If you're eighteen in April,
Or rising sixty-five,
When April comes to Amberley
With skies of April blue,
And Cotswold girls are briding
With slyly tilted shoe.

THOMAS YARNTON OF TARLTON
by John Drinkwater

The hamlet of Tarlton is very near Cirencester.

One of those old men fearing no man,
Two hundred broods his eaves have known
Since they cut on a Sapperton churchyard
stone –
" Thomas Yarnton of Tarlton, Yeoman."

At dusk you can hear the yeomen calling
The cattle still to Sapperton stalls,
And still the stroke of the woodman falls
As Thomas of Tarlton heard it falling.

I walked these meadows in seventeen-hundred,
Seed of his loins, a dream that stirred
Beyond the shape of a yeoman's word,
So faint that but unawares he wondered.

And now, from the weeds of his tomb uncomely,
I travel again the tracks he made,
And walks at my side the yeoman shade
Of Thomas Yarnton of Tarlton dumbly.

THE COW IN APPLE TIME
by Robert Frost

Although an American, Robert Frost, 1874-1963, is included here due to his association with the Cotswolds and the 'Dymock poets'. While living in Great Britain from 1912 to 1915, Frost and his family had rented a cottage, Little Iddens, near Dymock, Gloucestershire. Surrounded by his peers, Frost wrote some of his best work here, including this portrait of a cow gorging on windfall apples.

Something inspires the only cow of late
To make no more of a wall than an open gate,
And think no more of wall-builders than fools.
Her face is flecked with pomace and she drools
A cider syrup. Having tasted fruit,
She scorns a pasture withering to the root.
She runs from tree to tree where lie and sweeten.
The windfalls spiked with stubble and worm-eaten.
She leaves them bitten when she has to fly.
She bellows on a knoll against the sky.
Her udder shrivels and the milk goes dry.

THE ROAD NOT TAKEN
by Robert Frost

Robert Frost began writing this, one of his best-loved poems, in Gloucestershire. Although open to differing interpretations, Frost said that the poem began as a gentle satire on his close friend and fellow poet Edward Thomas with whom he used to take countryside walks. Upon returning from their walks, Thomas often expressed a wish that they had taken an alternate path.

Two roads diverged in a yellow wood,
And sorry I could not travel both
And be one traveler, long I stood
And looked down one as far as I could
To where it bent in the undergrowth;

Then took the other, as just as fair
And having perhaps the better claim,
Because it was grassy and wanted wear;
Though as for that, the passing there
Had worn them really about the same,

And both that morning equally lay
In leaves no step had trodden black
Oh, I kept the first for another day!
Yet knowing how way leads on to way,
I doubted if I should ever come back.

I shall be telling this with a sigh
Somewhere ages and ages hence:
two roads diverged in a wood, and I -
I took the one less traveled by,
And that has made all the difference.

THE COTSWOLD FARMERS
by John Drinkwater

As well as being a successful poet and playwright, John Drinkwater was also a manager of the Birmingham Repertory Theatre.

Sometimes the ghosts forgotten go
Along the hill-top way,
And with long scythes of silver mow
Meadows of moonlit hay,
Until the cocks of Cotswold crow
The coming of the day.

There's Tony Turkletob who died
When he could drink no more,
And Uncle Heritage, the pride
of eighteen-twenty-four,
And Ebenezer Barleytide,
And others half a score.

They fold in phantom pens, and plough
Furrows without a share,
And one will milk a faery cow,
And one will stare and stare,
And whistle ghostly tunes that now
Are not sung anywhere.

The moon goes down on Oakridge lea,
The other world's astir,
The Cotswold Farmers silently
Go back to sepulchre,
The sleeping watchdogs wake, and see
No ghostly harvester.

COUNTRYSIDE AROUND DIXTON MANOR, CIRCA 1715[5]
by Ken Smith

Ken Smith, 1938-2003, was born in Rudston, Yorkshire, the son of a farm labourer. Here he examines the myth of the rural idyll.

> Now strike up drum
> come harvest man come.
> Blowe horne or sleapers
> and cheere up thy reapers
> (from *Five Hundred Points of Good Husbandry*, 1580, by Thomas Tusser)

Layer under layer under the paintwork
England is making its Midsummer hay –

the dancing morris, pipelads and drum,
scythemen and rakers, cockers and carters

and centrefield my lord with his ladies
riding where now the pylon hums

with its wires over spring wheat
through the early morning mist.

These are the same hedgebacks,
same lie to the landscape, Mickle Mead,

Barrowdine, Harp Field and Sausage
still here though the names gone now.

In oils, unsigned, anonymous, a jobber
moving through landscape, used maybe
the wide angle lens of the camera oscura
for this sweep of a corner of Gloustershire,

back when all was thought well enough,
and nothing would change beyond this –
these peasants sweating in harvest
content dreaming brown ale and a fumble

5. Countryside around Dixton Manor is the title of a huge painting by an anonymous artist, dated circa 1715, on view in Cheltenham Art Gallery.

among the haycocks, and the dancers dance off
to their drink and their shillings. My lord lies now
and since and soon and thereafter in Alderton
in St Mary of Antioch, long dead.

Long gone, nameless maids in a row,
long curve of the back of 23 men
in a Mexican wave of swung scythes

to their lost graves. Two gossips
by the gate that is still a gate
maybe went for infantry, and the pipeboy

shipped out to the far world, most
stayed, went hungry, died anyway.
The painting's a lie, the landscape true
where the field keeps its shape. Everything
beyond this moment is yet to happen.
Everyone here is part of the dust now.

If my heart aches it's for this
though none of it's true:

the world we have lost never was
so we never lost it:

glitter of horse brass, bells
rolling over the evening:

all my lord's dream of himself
in a hired man's painting:

same tale then as now
and this has not changed either:

the enrichment of the rich,
impoverishment of the poor.

None but the reaper
will come to your door.

EVENING
Anonymous

This uncredited poem appeared in Volume 21, number 2 of the Royal Agricultural College Journal, 1934.

I think the loveliest of all earthly things
Is a June night,
When the river moves and the trees are still,
And the stars, slow shining,
Watch from above
And tell the secret loves of men to the age old moon,
And she to the mountains.
When the grasses rest,
And evening has gathered in her silken basket
The shadows of light that fly about the waters,
And sleep calls all men to her breast,
So lovingly,
As a mother to her children:
Then is it my delight,
To watch the stillness;
To hear the silence;
And pray that my soul
Were ever so tranquil as the soul of Nature.

UP THERE
by Ivor Gurney

Ivor Gurney was born in Gloucester, and often walked the hills between Gloucester and Cheltenham.

On Cotswold edge there is a field and that
Grows thick with corn and speedwell and the mat
Of thistles, of the tall kind; Rome lived there,
Some hurt centurion got his grant or tenure,
Built farm with fowls and pigsties and wood-piles,
Waited for service custom between whiles.
The farmer ploughs up coins in the wet-earth time,
He sees them on the topple of crests gleam,
Or run down furrow; and halts and does let them lie
Like a small black island in brown immensity,
Red pottery easy discovered, no searching needed...
One wonders what farms were like, no searching needed,
As now the single kite hovering still
By the coppice there, level with the flat of the hill.

Trees and Woods

ASSEMBLING A TREE
by Mario Petrucci

Describing himself as a poet, ecologist and 'lapsed physicist', Mario Petrucci (born 1958) is passionate about moving between the disciplines and is active at the interfaces between science, ecology and poetry. His poetry lies at the heart of the award-winning 'Heavy Water: a film for Chernobyl' (Seventh Art, 2006) and 'Amazonia' (Natural History Museum, 2010).

(after Edwin Brock, 'Five Ways to Kill a Man')

There are many pointless ways to assemble a tree.
You can heave planks of wood
to a hilltop fort and nail them together. To do this
properly you require a crowd of
commentators carrying cameras, a stopwatch and one
bolt of lightning.

Or you can take a lengthy research project, shaped and
chased in an entrepreneurial way, boasting
the full set-up of alloy rods and electrified cages. But for
this you need blue-sky funding, not to mention
Parliamentary blind eyes, backhanders for questions, sole
backing of a Welsh Prince, a mess of laboratory
rats sprouting velvety leaves for ears and a considerable
sliver of luck.

Dispensing with that, you may, if the spirits allow, blow
life into a plastic one – but then you need
a thousand miles of microscopic capillary pumping artificial
sap, an inland ocean of hydroponic support,
nanotech solar panels hammered into little grey, ear-like ovals
and some green paint.

In an age of synthetic xylem, you may ply a billion sheets
to less than millimetre thickness to be
replaced (preferably) annually – a world of scientists
huddled round their totem sections
of ersatz trunk applying the pale waistcoats in time.
(Plus a patent xylem welder.)

These are, as I began, pointless ways to assemble a tree.
Squirrels and simpletons have taken a seed,
the living seed, sunk it in the middle of an open field
and left it there.

THE FORESTERS ARMS
by Anthony Thwaite

Anthony Thwaite was born in Chester in 1930 and lives in Norfolk. He was awarded the OBE in 1992, for services to poetry.

No trees in sight except thin spindly things
Giving no shelter to animal or bird,
Not worth the pruning, valueless as fuel,
Bearing no fruit or timber: concrete acreage
Stretches about, grey packaging of soil.
On the hill gradient no sound is heard
But lorries changing gear; no beat of wings
Of hawk or owl above this global village.
A tanker pumps in someone's Special Ale.

Scragged earth, starved grass, coke litter under rain,
Low sheds and railway sidings – factories
That ease my life with things I do not need
Dictate such stuff. And in among it all,
Its sign new painted, chrome replacing wood,
At odds with every neighbouring thing it sees,
The Foresters Arms marks out its old domain,
Deaf to the echo of a horn's long call
And sounds of men with axes felling trees.

ALL THAT'S PAST
by Walter de la Mare

Walter de la Mare, 1873-1956, was an English poet, short story writer and novelist.

Very old are the woods;
And the buds that break
Out of the brier's boughs,
When March winds wake,
So old with their beauty are -
Oh, no man knows
Through what wild centuries
Roves back the rose.

Very old are the brooks;
And the rills that rise
Where snow sleeps cold beneath
The azure skies
Sing such a history
Of come and gone,
Their every drop is as wise
As Solomon.

Very old are we men;
Our dreams are tales
Told in dim Eden
By Eve's nightingales;
We wake and whisper awhile,
But, the day gone by,
Silence and sleep like fields
Of amaranth lie.

LONDON PLANE
by Andrew Motion

Andrew Motion, born in 1952, read English at University College, Oxford, and later taught English at the University of Hull where he met the university librarian and poet Philip Larkin. Motion later went on to write Larkin's biography. He presided as Poet Laureate between 1999 and 2009.

They felled the plane that broke the pavement slabs.
My next-door neighbour worried for his house.
He said the roots had cracked his bedroom wall.
The Council sent tree-surgeons and he watched.
A thin man in the heat without a shirt.
They started at the top and then worked down.
It took a day with one hour free for lunch.
The trunk was carted off in useful logs.

The stump remained for two weeks after that.
A wren sat on it once.
Then back the tree-men came with their machine.
They chomped the stump and left a square of mud.
All afternoon the street was strewn with bits.
That night the wind got up and blew it bare.

TREES CANNOT NAME THE SEASONS
by Roger McGough

Roger McGough was awarded an OBE for services to poetry in 1997, and a CBE in 2004. He was also recently honoured with the Freedom of the City of Liverpool.

Trees cannot name the seasons
Nor flowers tell the time.
But when the sun shines
And they are charged with light,
They take a day-long breath.
What we call 'night'
Is their soft exhalation.

And when joints creak yet again
and the dead skin of leaves falls,
Trees don't complain
Nor mourn the passing of hours.
What we call 'winter'
Is simply hibernation.

And as continuation
Comes to them as no surprise
They feel no need
To divide and itemize.
Nature has never needed reasons
For flowers to tell the time
Or trees put a name to seasons.

THE FUTURE OF FORESTRY
by CS Lewis

Best known today for his Narnia stories for children, Clive Staples Lewis, 1898-1963, was also a close friend of JRR Tolkien. Both taught at Oxford University and were members of a literary group called 'The Inklings'.

How will the legend of the age of trees
Feel, when the last tree falls in England?
When the concrete spreads and the town conquers
The country's heart; when contraceptive
Tarmac's laid where farm has faded,
Tramline flows where slept a hamlet,
And shop-fronts, blazing without a stop from
Dover to Wrath, have glazed us over?
Simplest tales will then bewilder
The questioning children, "What was a chestnut?
Say what it means to climb a Beanstalk,
Tell me, grandfather, what an elm is.
What was Autumn? They never taught us."
Then, told by teachers how once from mould
Came growing creatures of lower nature
Able to live and die, though neither
Beast nor man, and around them wreathing
Excellent clothing, breathing sunlight –
Half understanding, their ill-acquainted
Fancy will tint their wonder-paintings
– Trees as men walking, wood-romances
Of goblins stalking in silky green,
Of milk-sheen froth upon the lace of hawthorn's
Collar, pallor in the face of birchgirl.
So shall a homeless time, though dimly
Catch from afar (for soul is watchful)
A sight of tree-delighted Eden.

THE WAY THROUGH THE WOODS
by Rudyard Kipling

Rudyard Kipling, 1865-1936, is perhaps most famous for The Jungle Book and the Just So Stories. He was born in India, though between the ages of 37 and 71 he lived at Bateman's in East Sussex, now owned by the National Trust. In fact he bought up 300 acres of surrounding farmland to ensure his privacy.

They shut the road through the woods
Seventy years ago.
Weather and rain have undone it again,
And now you would never know
There was once a road through the woods
Before they planted the trees.
It is underneath the coppice and heath,
And the thin anemones.
Only the keeper sees
That, where the ring-dove broods,
And the badgers roll at ease,
There was once a road through the woods.

Yet, if you enter the woods
Of a summer evening late,
When the night-air cools on the trout-ringed pools
Where the otter whistles his mate.
(They fear not men in the woods,
Because they see so few)
You will hear the beat of a horse's feet,
And the swish of a skirt in the dew,
Steadily cantering through
The misty solitudes,
As though they perfectly knew
The old lost road through the woods ...
But there is no road through the woods.

THE TREES
by Philip Larkin

Philip Larkin, 1922-1985, is regarded as one of the greatest poets of the latter half of the twentieth century. In 1955 Larkin became University Librarian at the University of Hull, a post he would hold until his death, and he produced much of his poetry during this period.

The trees are coming into leaf
Like something almost being said;
The recent buds relax and spread,
Their greenness is a kind of grief.

Is it that they are born again
And we grow old? No, they die too,
Their yearly trick of looking new
Is written down in rings of grain.

Yet still the unresting castles thresh
In fullgrown thickness every May.
Last year is dead, they seem to say,
Begin afresh, afresh, afresh.

LOVELIEST OF TREES, THE CHERRY NOW
by AE Housman

This poem by AE Housman is taken from The Shropshire Lad, his best known work.

Loveliest of trees, the cherry now
Is hung with bloom along the bough,
And stands about the woodland ride
Wearing white for Eastertide.

Now, of my three score years and ten,
Twenty will not come again,
And take from seventy springs a score,
It only leaves me fifty more.

And since to look at things in bloom
Fifty springs are little room,
About the woodlands I will go
To see the cherry hung with snow.

BINSEY POPLARS – FELLED 1879
by Gerard Manley Hopkins

Gerard Manley Hopkins was inspired to write this poem when an avenue of mighty poplars, each 100 feet high, along the bank of the Thames between Oxford and the village of Binsey, was cut down one day in 1879.

My aspens dear, whose airy cages quelled,
Quelled or quenched in leaves the leaping sun,
All felled, felled, are all felled;
Of a fresh and following folded rank
Not spared, not one
That swam or sank
On meadow and river and wind-wandering weed-winding bank.

O if we but knew what we do
When we delve or hew-
Hack and rack the growing green!
Since country is so tender
To touch, her being so slender,
That, like this sleek and seeing ball
But a prick will made no eye at all,
Where we, even where we mean
To mend her we end her,
When we hew or delve:
After-comers cannot guess the beauty been.
Ten or twelve, only ten or twelve
Strokes of havoc unselve
The sweet especial scene,
Rural scene, a rural scene,
Sweet especial rural scene.

TREES
by William Henry Davies

The Welsh-born William Henry Davies, after his tramping adventures, eventually settled in Nailsworth, Gloucestershire, where he died in 1940.

They ask me where the Temple stands,
And is the Abbey far from there;
They ask the way to old St. Paul's,
And where they'll find Trafalgar Square.

As I pass on with my one thought
To find a quiet place with trees,
I answer him, I answer her,
I answer one and all of these.

When I sit under a green tree,
Silent, and breathing all the while
As easy as a sleeping child,
And smiling with as soft a smile –

Then, as my brains begin to work,
This is the thought that comes to me:
Were such a peace more often mine,
I'd live as long as this green tree.

THE LISTENERS
by Walter de la Mare

This is Walter de la Mare's best known poem. Given the poem's air of mystery, it is not surprising that he was also a successful writer of ghost stories.

'Is there anybody there?' said the Traveller,
knocking on the moonlit door;
And his horse in the silence champed the grasses
Of the forest's ferny floor:
And a bird flew up out of the turret,
Above the Traveller's head
And he smote upon the door again a second time;
'Is there anybody there?' he said.
But no one descended to the Traveller;
No head from the leaf-fringed sill
Leaned over and looked into his grey eyes,
Where he stood perplexed and still.
But only a host of phantom listeners
That dwelt in the lone house then
Stood listening in the quiet of the moonlight
To that voice from the world of men:
Stood thronging the faint moonbeams on the dark stair,
That goes down to the empty hall,
Hearkening in an air stirred and shaken
By the lonely Traveller's call.
And he felt in his heart their strangeness,
Their stillness answering his cry,
While his horse moved, cropping the dark turf,
'Neath the starred and leafy sky;
For he suddenly smote on the door, even
Louder, and lifted his head:-
'Tell them I came, and no one answered,
That I kept my word,' he said.
Never the least stir made the listeners,
Though every word he spake
Fell echoing through the shadowiness of the still house

From the one man left awake:
Ay, they heard his foot upon the stirrup,
And the sound of iron on stone,
And how the silence surged softly backward,
When the plunging hoofs were gone.

GREEN MAN[6]
by Heather Harrison

Heather Harrison, born 1943, is a contemporary English poet.

Fleet in the forest,
leafshaken, wild in the wood,
flowers tousled in his hair,
garlanded with laurel and with ivy,
the Green Grotesque swoops out of stone and timber.
Locked in a church boss
his eyes start with alarm
at his enclosure. Brown priests agreed
to give his effigy a place.
That would bring the gaffers in,
the maids with May bandeaus,
the mothers full of fears and needing cures.

They could turn an eye
towards the old religion
while they received the new.
Christ nailed to a tree would keep their reverence
front facing; they could fringe
the altar of the new covenant with evergreen
with rosemary to sprig the nosegays left
under the wood-man's stare.
Needs are many and the winter cold,
best to placate all gods.
The Mediterranean Lord of Life
could promise them a warmer afterlife,
the Forest Sprite green leaves,
a yellow corn and a berried harvest.

6. The Green Man is an ancient forest deity, whose face is often to be found carved in wood or stone. He has also given his name to many British pubs.

Water and the Land

THE LAKE ISLE OF INNISFREE
by William Butler Yeats

William Butler Yeats, 1865-1939, was an Irish poet and dramatist. He wrote the following poem while in London, which felt far removed from his carefree boyhood in rural County Sligo. Innisfreee is an uninhabited island in Lough Gill.

I will arise and go now, and go to Innisfree,
And a small cabin build there, of clay and wattles made:
Nine bean-rows will I have there, a hive for the honeybee,
And live alone in the bee-loud glade.

And I shall have some peace there, for peace comes dropping slow,
Dropping from the veils of the morning to where the cricket sings;
There midnight's all a-glimmer, and noon a purple glow,
And evening full of the linnet's wings.

I will arise and go now, for always night and day
I hear lake water lapping with low sounds by the shore;
While I stand on the roadway, or on the pavements gray,
I hear it in the deep heart's core.

SALMON
by Kenneth Steven

Kenneth Steven, born 1968, has lived most of his adult life in Highland Perthshire. He has said that almost all of his writing takes its inspiration from the land.

You are the Atlantic, the personification of
currents and spates,
You are made of fathoms of water,
Spring runs, Highland rivers –
You have your life's journey ravelled inside you.

I have been to stand on rock ledges
In the fierce rains of autumn;
I have looked down on kettledrums of river
Tumbled to white noise –

And there, up out of this tantrum,
You leap, pouring the source of your being,
The blunt thrust of your head,
Into an impossible return, the river's beginning.

THE RIVER
by Kathleen Raine

Kathleen Raine, 1908-2003, was a British poet, critic and scholar. She spent some of her childhood in a Northumberland village, and the idyllic nature of that upbringing had a great effect upon her, as indicated by the title of the first part of her autobiography, Farewell Happy Fields.

In my first sleep
I came to the river
And looked down
Through the clear water -
Only in dream
Water so pure,
Laced and undulant
Lines of flow
On its rocky bed
Water of life
Streaming for ever.

A house was there
Beside the river
And I, arrived,
An expected guest
About to explore
Old gardens and libraries -
But the car was waiting
To drive me away.

One last look
Into that bright stream -
Trout there were
And clear on the bottom
Monster form
Of the great crayfish
That crawls to the moon.
On its rocky bed
Living water

In whorls and ripples
Flowing unbended.

There was the car
To drive me away.
We crossed the river
Of living water –
I might not stay,
But must return
By the road too short
To the waiting day.

In my second dream
Pure I was and free
By the rapid stream,
My crystal house the sky,
The pure crystalline sky.

Into the stream I flung
A bottle of clear glass
That twirled and tossed and spun
In the water's race
Flashing the morning sun.

Down that swift river
I saw it borne away,
My empty crystal form,
Exultant saw it caught
Into the current's spin,
The flashing water's run.

ANGLER
by Adrian Henri

A member of the 'Liverpool poets', Adrian Henri, 1932-2000, was also a painter and member of the poetry-rock group 'The Liverpool Scene'.

His waders among the watercrowfoot,
intent behind his sunglasses, he casts repeatedly,
does not see me pass.

I sit
on the riverbank, see the meadowsweet,
agrimony, remembered dragonflies,
hear the water break the channel, cast about
for words.

Later
he trudges past, his creel
empty, sees my empty
notebook, smiles a secret smile
of complicity.

SIBARD'S WELL
by Charles Causley

Charles Causley returns again to his Cornish roots in Launceston for inspiration for this poem.

My house, named for the Saxon spring,
Stands by the sour farmyard, the long –
Dry lip that once was Sibard's Well
Buried beneath a winding-stone
To stop the cattle falling in;
Yet underfoot is still the sound
At last of night, at first of day,
In country silences, a thin
Language of water through the clay.

At mornings, in small light, I hear
Churn-clink, the bucket handle fall.
An iron shirt, a sudden spear
Unprop themselves from the farm wall.
A voice, in a far, altered speech
Beneath my window seems to say,
'I too lived here. I too awoke
In quarter light, when life's cold truth
Was all too clear. As clearly spoke.'

THE SPRING AT CHEDWORTH
by Alison Brackenbury

Alison Brackenbury, born 1953, lives in Gloucestershire. The following poem could also be in the Cotswolds section, since the Roman villa and sacred spring described here are in Chedworth, just outside Cirencester.

There is no goddess in the spring
the sturdy walls are bare.
The painted plaster crumbled
colours danced into the air.
The Victorian explorers
found their nymph no longer there.

She would not wait to greet them
though her mouth was never still.
Her baths, where girls sat idly
They miscalled a fulling mill.
'Nymphaeum'[7] fades their labels
where the empty waters spill.

I have seen her in the August yard,
shriek, beneath the hose,
leap in a Welsh river
in her rough and sweat-streaked clothes.
But desire runs through her fingers
she is gone as water goes.

She left inside her basin
a black beetle which clasps tight
a bead of air, her glistening gift,
as he spirals, out of sight,
as the cuckoo in the wet trees
as her laughter in the night.

7. A spring dedicated to a water nymph in ancient times.

WATERING PLACE
by Paul Hyland

Paul Hyland, born 1947, is an award winning poet and travel writer.

From pastureland I once dropped down
through a steep wood to where the sun
stopped in deep leaves before it lit
the floor, though a stream gathered it
and drew me, straying child, toward
music that light and water made ...
I found the carcass of a ram
fallen across it, a queer dam;
dead weight, soft fleece of washing wool,
grub-addled matter in its shell.
With adult sense there on the brink
I dared to stoop, upstream, and drink.
But since, wading in sleep, I've fled
headlong, parched, sick, hoping to tread
water where nothing died, a source,
untarnished tarn where sheer falls slice
into iced water, mirrored heaven.
I'll not dip there awake. As then
I must cup hands close to the rot,
upstream, just, where the water's sweet.

FIVE RIVERS
by Norman Nicholson

The poetry of Norman Nicholson, 1914-1987, is inextricably linked with the area of Cumbria on the edge of the Lake District where he lived all his life.

Southward from Whitehaven, where cliffs of coal
Slant like shale to the low black mole,
The railway canters along the curving shore
Over five rivers, which slowly pour
On the steps of the shingle where the grey gulls bask
EHEN and CALDER, IRT and MITE and ESK.

The EHEN twists and flicks its fin
Red as rhubarb beneath the grey skin,
For its veins are stained with the blood of the ore
Of the mines of Egremont and Cleator Moor.
Here drill and navvy break the stone
And hack the living earth to the bone;
Blood spurts like water from the stricken rock.
Seeps into drain and gully and trickles to the beck.
Green herringbones of watercresses ride
On the tilt and tug of the red tide;
Bladderwrack, thrift and salty turf
Crust over cobbles at the edge of the pink surf.

The introspective CALDER hums to the pebbles
A memory of plainsong and choirboys' trebles,
Of collect and introit, creed and antiphon,
Of cistercians in the abbey of blood-red stone,
Where now tarpaulin and sheet lead shield
Groined roof and cloister and stoup from the wild
Weather of time, and the wall ferns spread
Where once the praying lamp hung before the holy bread.

The IRT comes from Wastdale, the land of the screes,
Of bracken up to your waist and ham-and-egg teas,

Of men who remember Will Ritson, the biggest liar
That ever lived, who sit by the fire
And laugh their inherited laughs at the talk
Of hounds with wings of eagles sniffing the lake.

The MITE, the tyke, lollops along
Like a blue-haired collie with a dribbling tongue,
The children's plaything as they ride the toy train
That runs beneath the rocks in a hawthorn lane,
Where dog daisy, dogrose and stiff dog-grass
Bark at the wheels as the whistling truckloads pass.

But the ESK comes from the narrowest dale
Where statesmen meet at the Woolpack for a glass of ale
And a crack about herdwicks or a cure for the tick
And how some fool has broken his neck on the rock.
The ESK knows the stonechat and the parsley fern
And breaks like a bottle at every turn,
And bursts on the boulders and froths like beer,
Runs solid as glass and green and clear,
Till it mixes with MITE and IRT in the marsh,
Where roman cement and arches teach
Of the galleys that came to Ravenglass
Bearing the invaders with helmets of brass.
Where the plover creaks and the curlew whines,
The rivers ferret among the dunes,
Till the channels burst through a gap in the sand
Like a three pronged pitchfork jabbed in the flank of the land.

Brown clouds are blown against the bright fells
Like celtic psalms from drowned western isles.
The slow rain falls like memory
And floods the becks and flows to the sea,
And there on the coast of Cumberland mingle
The fresh and the salt, and the cinders and the shingle.

FROGS IN THE WOOD
by Brian Patten

As a performance poet and as a writer of poems for children and adults, Brian Patten is wary of intellectual analysis of his poetry.

How good it would be to be lost again,
Night falling on the compass and the map
Turning to improbable flames,
Bright ashes going out in the ponds.

And how good it would be
To stand bewildered in a strange wood
Where you are the loudest thing,
Your heart making a deafening noise.

And how strange when your fear of being lost has subsided
To stand listening to the frogs holding
Their arguments in the streams,
Condemning the barbarous herons.

And how right it is
To shrug off real and invented grief
As of no importance
To this moment of your life,

When being lost seems
So much more like being found,
And you find all that is lost
Is what weighed you down.

Birds and Animals of the Countryside

BARN OWL

by James Simpson

James Simpson, born 1968, has always lived in the South Downs, and his work is deeply rooted in the area.

I found the Owl shattered on the road
All bone and feathers
talons clenched
white ghost bloodied.

From the eaves of the crook barn
stink of straw and trampled corn
it would come at night,
snow flurry against a blackened cloud,
wraith companion of squalls and heavy sky.

And now I find
that the head hangs limp,
and the eye turns smoke
and stares.

HORSES AT CHRISTMAS
by Henry Shukman

Henry Shukman was born in Oxford in 1962. Besides producing travel writing and poetry he has also been a musician and trawlerman.

In our little house Creedence were singing
about the old cotton fields, the baby
was flat on his back in front of the fire,
eyes swimming with flame.
Christmas morning, and you were at church.
I thought of going to join you late,
but instead took the baby up to the horses.
Out in the field he started crying.
Maybe I should have taken him to the bath
of stone, the discipline of a saviour, the sanctuary
of hymns –
                                        But the horses saved us.
To be close to them, so tough and nothing
to do with us, and they breathing all over him,
and the flaking mud on their necks
where they had rolled, and the sucking of hooves
as they walked the sodden field.
The horses with their long heads,
underwater eyes, watched us watch them.
Then they turned, drumming the field,
leaving us alone – the damp morning
all about, the soaked grass under foot,
the baby's diaphanous ears going pink in the cold
as silence bowed back to earth.

TWELVE-POINTER STAG (extract from The Naturalist)
by Margaret Reynolds

This extract originally appeared in a Forestry Commission Guide first published in 1939.

To call a bird a bird, a tree a tree
Is insufficient for his earnest mind –
These words are symbols only, mute and blind.
Shape, colour, texture, sound identify
A bird, a tree, a singing in the air
Precisely. From a feather he restores
Heartbeat and cry and dappled spread of wing;
From slender lizard's imprint on the grass
His careful mind can reconstruct and bring
The shadows back, and see the creature there.

FARM ANIMALS
by Adrian Mitchell

Adrian Mitchell, 1932-2008, was an English poet, novelist and playwright. He was a lifelong pacifist.

Clotted cream sheep
We troop in a dream
Through the steep deep wool
Of a yellow meadow
We are oblong and boring
We are all alike
Liking to be all alike

And the grass-like grass
Is alike, all alike, and all we think
Is grass grass grass
Yes grass is all we think
And all we do
Is wool

But that's the deal, the ancient deal,
The wonderful deal between sheep and men

Men give grass
We come across with wool

That agreement was signed
On the green baize table in Eden

What would happen if we broke the contract?
Oh that would be mutiny, we would be punished
By being eaten, we would deserve to be eaten.
But of course we never rebel, so we are never eaten.

COW IN CALF
by Seamus Heaney

Seamus Heaney's use of striking similes really helps to recreate this moment of drama for the reader.

It seems she has swallowed a barrel.
From forelegs to haunches
her belly is slung like a hammock.

Slapping her out of the byre is like slapping
a great bag of seed. My hand
tingled as if strapped, but I had to
hit her again and again and
heard the blows plump like a depth-charge
far in her gut.

The udder grows. Windbags
of bagpipes are crammed there
to drone in her lowing.
Her cud and her milk, her heats[8] and her calves
keep coming and going.

8. Probably a reference to the cow's ability to breed several times throughout the year.

DEER
by John Burnside

John Burnside, born 1955, is a Scottish poet and novelist. He lived for a while in Gloucestershire, and has been described as a poet of 'the open air'.

> 'of your charity disturb them not
> in their Arcadia'
> F Fraser Darling

Coming inside from a meal
in the garden, the lights burning out
on the table, a threadlike spill
of maple syrup warming in the dark
to draw some passing creature to this quiet
theatre of crockery and fruit bowls and the last glimmer
of chablis amongst the pears,

we wonder about those legends
of women transformed into deer,
or a cold daughter, lost in the hills
and hidden in the caught breath of a fawn.

Imagine how they slip between two lives
in skipping rhymes; how they recall
the water in the fern, or wintersweet
unfurling on the tongue's unfinished skin;
how, when they steal in through the cypress hedge
to such a feast, they catch a thread of musk
and see themselves again, in human form.

Sometimes have waited at the edge
of darkness for a glimpse of something wild
and mutable, a sweet glitch in the tale
to show the borderland through which they pass,

and if could have chosen anything
but this inevitable self, I'd be the one
who walks alone and barefoot in the woods

to stand, amidst a family of deer,
knowing her kind, and knowing the chasm between
one presence and the next as nothing more
than something learned, like memory or song.

THE DARKLING THRUSH
by Thomas Hardy

This lyrical poem by Thomas Hardy, 1840-1928, was originally to have been called The Century's End, 1900, and it can be read as symbolic of the poet's hope for a new century.

I leant upon a coppice gate
When Frost was spectre-gray,
And Winter's dregs made desolate
The weakening eye of day.

The tangled bine-stems scored the sky
Like strings of broken lyres,
And all mankind that haunted nigh
Had sought their household fires.

The land's sharp features seem'd to be
The Century's corpse outleant,
His crypt the cloudy canopy,
The wind his death-lament.
The ancient pulse of germ and birth
Was shrunken hard and dry,
And every spirit upon earth
Seem'd fervourless as I.

At once a voice arose among
The bleak twigs overhead
In a full-hearted evensong
Of joy illimited;
An aged thrush, frail, gaunt, and small,
In blast-beruffled plume,
Had chosen thus to fling his soul
Upon the growing gloom.

So little cause for carollings
Of such ecstatic sound
Was written on terrestrial things

Afar or nigh around,
That I could think there trembled through
His happy good-night air
Some blessèd Hope, whereof he knew
And I was unaware.

The Darker Side

THE BADGER
by John Clare

John Clare, 1793-1864 was the son of a farm labourer. He lived at the time when the Agricultural Revolution was taking place, and he was deeply distressed by the loss of the old way of life. Nevertheless, the following poem is not in the least bit sentimental.

When midnight comes a host of dogs and men
Go out and track the badger to his den,
And put a sack within the hole, and lie
Till the old grunting badger passes by.
He comes and hears – they let the strongest loose.
The old fox gears the noise and drops the goose.
The poacher shoots and hurries from the cry,
And the old hare half wounded buzzes by.
They get a forked stick to bear him down
And clap the dogs and take him to the town,
And bait him all the day with many dogs,
And laugh and shout and fright the scampering hogs.
He runs along and bites at all he meets:
They shout and hollo down the noisy streets.

He turns about to face the loud uproar
And drives the rebels to their very door.
The frequent stone is hurled where'er they go;
When badgers fight, then everyone's a foe.
The dogs are clapped and urged to join the fray;
The badger turns and drives them all away.
Though scarcely half as big, demure and small,
He fights with dogs for hours and beats them all.
The heavy mastiff, savage in the fray,
Lies down and licks his feet and turns away.
The bulldog knows his match and waxes cold,
The badger grins and never leaves his hold.
He drives the crowd and follows at their heels
And bites them through – the drunkard swears and reels

The frighted women take the boys away,
The blackguard laughs and hurries on the fray.
He tries to reach the woods, and awkward race,
But sticks and cudgels quickly stop the chase.
He turns again and drives the noisy crowd
And beats the many dogs in noises loud.
He drives away and beats them every one,
And then they loose them all and set them on.
He falls as dead and kicked by boys and men,
Then starts and grins and drives the crowd again;
Till kicked and torn and beaten out he lies
And leaves his hold and crackles, groans, and dies.

THE WELSH HILL COUNTRY
by RS Thomas

Here Ronald Stuart Thomas ruthlessly dissects the idealised view that tourists may have of rural Wales.

Too far for you to see
The fluke and the foot-rot and the fat maggot
Gnawing the skin from the small bones,
The sheep are grazing at Bwlch-y-Fedwen,
Arranged romantically in the usual manner
On a bleak background of bald stone.

Too far for you to see
The moss and the mould on the cold chimneys,
The nettles growing through the cracked doors,
The houses stand empty at Nant-yr-Eira,
There are holes in the roofs that are thatched with sunlight,
And the fields are reverting to the bare moor.

Too far, too far to see
The set of his eyes and the slow pthisis[9]
Wasting his frame under the ripped coat,
There's a man still farming at Ty'n-y-Fawnog,
Contributing grimly to the accepted pattern,
The embryo music dead in his throat.

9. A term used to refer to a wasting disease such as tuberculosis.

TWO PHEASANTS
by Michael Longley

Michael Longley, born 1939, is a contemporary Irish poet whose work is influenced by the landscape and wildlife of Ireland.

As though from a catastrophic wedding reception
The cock pheasant in his elaborate waistcoat
Exploded over cultivated ground to where
A car in front of our car had crushed his bride.

I got the picture in no time in my wing-mirror
As in a woodcut by Hokusai who highlighted
The head for me, the white neck-ring and red wattles,
The long coppery tail, the elegance and pain.

BARROW
by John Greening

John Greening, born 1954, is a poet, playwright, critic and creative writing tutor.

Our brittle bones were chilled to envy
even of the bones in Stoney Littleton
Long Barrow, where I had tapped

at a tubercular farmhouse to beg
and stood awaiting something at the entrance
to a chamber, sealed and on the list

for surgery. But there was no key.
And since our torch was not charged up, we
gazed down a narrow beam of darkness

imagining ourselves through there, to turn
and find this glow, as – looking back –
one might spot brilliance in a dark age.

Across the valley, the sun quite lost
in a serge grey labyrinth, a whole field
once filled with hay is landfill now:

yellow skips, black plastic, keening
white gulls, and us – powerless
above our age's burial mound.

ON BEING ASKED TO WRITE A SCHOOL HYMN
by Charles Causley

The poems of Charles Causley, born the only child of a groom and gardener, were inspired by folk songs, ballads and hymns.

On a starless night and still
Underneath a sleeping hill
Comes the cry of sheep and kine
From the slaughter house to mine.

Fearful is the call and near
Though I do not want to hear,
Though it has been said by some
That the animal is dumb.

Gone the byre and gone the breeze
And the gently moving trees
As with stabbing eye they run
In a clear, electric sun.

Now, red-fingered to their trade
With the shot and with the blade,
Rubber-booted angels white
Enter as the morning light.

But who wields that knife and gun
Does not strike the blow alone,
And there is no place to stand
Other than at his right hand.

God, who does not dwell on high
In the wide, unwinking sky,
And whose quiet counsels start
Simply from the human heart,

Teach us strong and teach us true
What to say and what to do,
That we love as best we can
All Thy creatures. Even man.
Amen

HARVEST HYMN
by John Betjeman

This poem by John Betjeman, 1906-1984, is a clever parody of the harvest hymn, 'We plough the fields and scatter the good seed on the land'.

We spray the fields and scatter
The poison on the ground
So that no wicked wild flowers
Upon our farm be found.
We like whatever helps us
To line our purse with pence;
The twenty-four-hour broiler-house
And neat electric fence.

All concrete sheds around us
And Jaguars in the yard,
The telly lounge and deep-freeze
Are ours from working hard.

We fire the fields for harvest,
The hedges swell the flame,
The oak trees and the cottages
From which our fathers came.
We give no compensation,
The earth is ours today,
And if we lose on arable,
Then bungalows will pay.

All concrete sheds around us
And Jaguars in the yard,
The telly lounge and deep-freeze
Are ours from working hard.

TO THE MEN OF ENGLAND
by Percy Bysshe Shelley

Percy Bysshe Shelley, 1792-1822, one of the major English Romantic poets, was also the most radical in his views and was a strong advocate for social justice. He was married to Mary Shelley, the author of Frankenstein.

Men of England, wherefore plough
For the lords who lay ye low?
Wherefore weave with toil and care
The rich robes your tyrants wear?

Wherefore feed and clothe and save,
From the cradle to the grave,
Those ungrateful drones who would
Drain your sweat – nay, drink your blood?

Wherefore, Bees of England, forge
Many a weapon, chain, and scourge,
That these stingless drones may spoil
The forced produce of your toil?

Have ye leisure, comfort, calm,
Shelter, food, love's gentle balm?
Or what is it ye buy so dear
With your pain and with your fear?

The seed ye sow another reaps;
The wealth ye find another keeps;
The robes ye weave another wears;
The arms ye forge another bears.

Sow seed, – but let no tyrant reap;
Find wealth, – let no imposter heap;
Weave robes, – let not the idle wear;
Forge arms, in your defence to bear.

Shrink to your cellars, holes, and cells;
In halls ye deck another dwells.

Why shake the chains ye wrought? Ye see
The steel ye tempered glance on ye.

With plough and spade and hoe and loom,
Trace your grave, and build your tomb,
And weave your winding-sheet, till fair
England be your sepulchre!

RENEWAL OF THE LAND

THE SEED SHOP
by Muriel Stuart

Muriel Stuart, 1885-1967, was a highly praised poet, but she eventually gave up the writing of poetry to concentrate on her love of gardening. She wrote two gardening books, the second of which, called Gardener's Nightcap, is still in print.

Here in a quiet and dusty room they lie,
Faded as crumbled stone or shifting sand,
Forlorn as ashes, shrivelled, scentless, dry -
Meadows and gardens running through my hand.

In this brown husk a dale of hawthorn dreams;
A cedar in this narrow cell is thrust
That will drink deeply of a century's streams;
These lilies shall make summer on my dust.

Here in their safe and simple house of death,
Sealed in their shells, a million roses leap;
Here I can blow a garden with my breath,
And in my hand a forest lies asleep.

THE HORSES
by Edwin Muir

Edwin Muir, 1887-1959, was born on a farm in Deerness on the Orkney Islands where he lived happily until rising farm rents forced the family to move to Glasgow. This loss of an idyllic rural childhood had a profound effect on Muir.

Barely a twelvemonth after
The seven days war that put the world to sleep,
Late in the evening the strange horses came.
By then we had made our covenant with silence,
But in the first few days it was so still
We listened to our breathing and were afraid.
On the second day
The radios failed; we turned the knobs; no answer.
On the third day a warship passed us, heading north,
Dead bodies piled on the deck. On the sixth day
A plane plunged over us into the sea. Thereafter
Nothing. The radios dumb;
And still they stand in corners of our kitchens,
And stand, perhaps, turned on, in a million rooms
All over the world. But now if they should speak,
If on a sudden they should speak again,
If on the stroke of noon a voice should speak,
We would not listen, we would not let it bring
That old bad world that swallowed its children quick
At one great gulp. We would not have it again.
Sometimes we think of the nations lying asleep,
Curled blindly in impenetrable sorrow,
And then the thought confounds us with its strangeness.
The tractors lie about our fields; at evening
They look like dank sea-monsters couched and waiting.
We leave them where they are and let them rust:
'They'll molder away and be like other loam.'
We make our oxen drag our rusty plows,
Long laid aside. We have gone back
Far past our fathers' land.

And then, that evening
Late in the summer the strange horses came.
We heard a distant tapping on the road,
A deepening drumming; it stopped, went on again
And at the corner changed to hollow thunder.
We saw the heads
Like a wild wave charging and were afraid.
We had sold our horses in our fathers' time
To buy new tractors. Now they were strange to us
As fabulous steeds set on an ancient shield.
Or illustrations in a book of knights.
We did not dare go near them. Yet they waited,
Stubborn and shy, as if they had been sent
By an old command to find our whereabouts
And that long-lost archaic companionship.
In the first moment we had never a thought
That they were creatures to be owned and used.
Among them were some half a dozen colts
Dropped in some wilderness of the broken world,
Yet new as if they had come from their own Eden.
Since then they have pulled our plows and borne our loads
But that free servitude still can pierce our hearts.
Our life is changed; their coming our beginning.

SCATTERING THE ASHES
by Grevel Lindop

Grevel Lindop, born 1948, is an English poet, academic and literary critic.

At last the rain cleared and we found a barley-field
where the crop was knee-high, and in our town shoes
paced the lumpy furrows along the edge
until our trousers were soaked. My brother held it out,
open, and I pushed my hand in. It was like
dark corn, or oatmeal, or both, the fine dust
surprisingly heavy as it sighed through the green
blades and hit the earth. And like the sower
in that nursery picture ('To bed with the lamb,
and up with the laverock[10]') we strode on, flinging it
broadcast, left and right, out over the field.
And there was no doubt that things were all in their places,
the tumbled clouds moving back, light in the wheel-ruts
and puddles of the lane as we walked to the car;
and yes, there were larks scribbling their songs on the sky
as the air warmed up. We noticed small steps
by a pool in the stream where a boy might have played
and people fetched water once, and wild watercress
that streamed like green hair inside the ribbed gloss of the current.
And then I was swinging the wheel as we found our way
round the lane corners in a maze of tall hedges
patched with wild roses, under steep slopes of larch
and sycamore, glimpsing the red sandstone of castles
hidden high in the woods. And the grit under our nails
was the midpoint of a spectrum that ran from the pattern in our cells
to the memories of two children, and it was all right.

10. A Scots word for skylark.

THE YEAR'S AWAKENING
by Thomas Hardy

Thomas Hardy is still best known for his novels such as Tess of the D'Urbervilles and Far from the Madding Crowd, though his poetry has become increasingly well-regarded. A number of them show a love for, and keen observation of, the natural world.

How do you know that the pilgrim track
Along the belting zodiac
Swept by the sun in his seeming rounds
Is traced by now to the Fishes' bounds
And into the Ram, when weeks of cloud
Have wrapt the sky in a clammy shroud,
And never as yet a tinct of spring
Has shown in the Earth's apparelling;
O vespering bird, how do you know,
How do you know?

How do you know, deep underground,
Hid in your bed from sight and sound,
Without a turn in temperature,
With weather life can scarce endure,
That light has won a fraction's strength,
And day put on some moments' length,
Whereof in merest rote will come,
Weeks hence, mild airs that do not numb;
O crocus root, how do you know,
How do you know?

ALL NATURE HAS A FEELING
by John Clare

John Clare continued to write poetry until his death at the age of 71, despite suffering increasingly from mental health problems.

All nature has a feeling: woods, fields, brooks
Are life eternal: and in silence they
Speak happiness beyond the reach of books;
There's nothing mortal in them; their decay
Is the green life of change; to pass away
And come again in blooms revivified.
Its birth was heaven, eternal is its stay,
And with the sun and moon shall still abide
Beneath their day and night and heaven wide.

THE BURNING OF THE LEAVES
by Laurence Binyon

The poet and art historian Laurence Binyon, 1869-1943, is today best remembered for his poem For the Fallen that is often recited at Remembrance Sunday services. It includes the lines: 'They shall grow not old, as we that are left grow old: / Age shall not weary them, nor the years condemn. / At the going down of the sun and in the morning, / We will remember them'. Like many of the English War poets, his work is often deeply rooted in the English landscape.

Now is the time for the burning of the leaves.
They go to the fire; the nostril pricks with smoke
Wandering slowly into a weeping mist.
Brittle and blotched, ragged and rotten sheaves!
A flame siezes the smouldering ruin and bites
On stubborn stalks that crackle as they resist.

The last hollyhock's fallen tower is dust;
All the spices of June are a bitter reek,
All the extravagant riches spent and mean.
All burns! The reddest rose is a ghost;
Sparks whirl up, to expire in the mist: the wild
Fingers of fire are making corruption clean.

Now is the time for stripping the spirit bare,
Time for the burning of days ended and done.
Idle solace of things that have gone before:
Rootless hope and fruitless desire are there;
Let them go to the fire, with never a look behind.
The world that was ours is a world that is ours no more.

They will come again, the leaf and the flower, to arise
From squalor of rottenness into the old splendour,
And magical scents to a wondering memory bring;
The same glory, to shine upon different eyes.
Earth cares for her own ruins, naught for ours.
Nothing is certain, only the certain spring.

AND DID THOSE FEET IN ANCIENT TIME (Jerusalem)
by William Blake

William Blake, 1757-1827, was a visionary poet, painter, and printmaker. This short poem (a preface to a much longer work) makes reference to the legend that a young Jesus, accompanied by his uncle Joseph of Arimathea, travelled to England and visited Glastonbury. He contrasts this vision of an earthly paradise with the effects of the Industrial Revolution and its 'dark satanic mills'.

And did those feet in ancient time
Walk upon England's mountains green?
And was the holy Lamb of God
On England's pleasant pastures seen?

And did the Countenance Divine
Shine forth upon our clouded hills?
And was Jerusalem builded here
Among these dark satanic mills?

Bring me my bow of burning gold!
Bring me my arrows of desire!
Bring me my spear! O clouds, unfold!
Bring me my chariot of fire!

I will not cease from mental fight,
Nor shall my sword sleep in my hand,
Till we have built Jerusalem
In England's green and pleasant land.

INDEX OF POETS

SOURCES AND ACKNOWLEDGEMENTS

Poet and poem(s)	*Acknowledgements*	*Source*
Armitage, Simon *Millet: the Gleaners*	Reproduced by kind permission of Faber & Faber Ltd.	*Kid*, pub. Faber & Faber, 1992.
Betjeman, John *Harvest Hymn*	Copyright © The Estate of John Betjeman 1955, 1958, 1962, 1964, 1968, 1970, 1979, 1981, 1982, 2001. Reproduced by permission of John Murray (Publishers).	*Collected Poems.*
Binyon, Laurence *The Burning of the Leaves*	Reproduced by kind permission of the Society of Authors as the literary representatives of the Estate of Laurence Binyon.	
Blunden, Edmund *Forefathers*	Reproduced by kind permission of the author and Carcanet Press Ltd.	*Selected Poems*, pub. Carcanet Press, 1993.
Brackenbury, Alison *The Spring at Chedworth*	Reproduced by kind permission of the author and Carcanet Press Ltd.	*1829*, pub. Carcanet Press, 1995.
Burnside, John *Deer*	Reprinted by kind permission of The Random House Group Ltd.	*The Light Trap*, pub. Jonathan Cape, 2002.
Causley, Charles *I Saw a Jolly Hunter* *Sibard's Well* *On Being Asked to Write a School Hymn*	Reproduced by kind permission of David Higham Associates Limited.	*Collected Poems*, pub. Macmillan.
Davies, William Henry *Leisure* *Trees*	Reproduced by kind permission of Kieron Griffin as Trustee of Mrs HM Davies Will Trust.	
de la Mare, Walter *All That's Past* *The Listeners*	Reproduced by kind permission of The Literary Trustees of Walter de la Mare and the Society of Authors as their representative.	*The Complete Poems of Walter de la Mare.*
Duffy, Maureen *Burning Off*	Copyright © Maureen Duffy 1985. Reprinted by kind permission of Jonathan Clowes Ltd., London, on behalf of Maureen Duffy.	*Collected Poems 1949-84*, pub. Hamish Hamilton, 1985.
Edwards, Justin (writing as Perkin Warrant) *But the times, they may be a-changing*	Reproduced by kind permission of Cheryl Hayes Management.	*The Odd Half Hour*, BBC Radio 4.

Eliot, Thomas Stearns *Little Gidding*	Reproduced by kind permission of Faber & Faber Ltd.	*Four Quartets*, pub. Faber & Faber, 1944.
Frost, Robert *The Cow in Apple Time* *The Road Not Taken*	Reprinted by kind permission of The Random House Group Ltd.	*The Poetry of Robert Frost,* edited by Edward Connery Lathem, pub. Jonathan Cape.
Greening, John *Barrow*	Reproduced by kind permission of Shoestring Press.	
Groarke, Vona *Thistle*	Reproduced by kind permission of The Gallery Press.	*Flight*, pub. The Gallery Press, 2002.
Hamburger, Michael *Bread and Butter Letter*	Reproduced by kind permission of Anvil Press Poetry.	*Collected Poems 1941-1994*, pub. Anvil Press, 1995.
Harrison, Heather *Green Man*	The editors have been unsuccessful in tracing right(s) holders.	*Beneath the Pavement,* 1987.
Heaney, Seamus *Follower* *Blackberry Picking* *Cow in Calf*	Reproduced by kind permission of Faber & Faber Ltd.	*Opened Ground: Poems 1966-1996* by Seamus Heaney, pub. Faber & Faber, 2002
Henri, Adrian *Angler*	Copyright © Adrian Henri. Reproduced by kind permission of the estate of Adrian Henri c/o Rogers, Coleridge & White Ltd., 20 Powis Mews, London W11 1JN.	*The Best of Adrian Henri.*
Hughes, Ted *Thistles*	Reproduced by kind permission of Faber & Faber Ltd.	*Collected Poems*, pub. Faber & Faber, 2003.
Hyland, Paul *Watering Place*	Reproduced by kind permission of David Higham Associates Limited.	*The art of the impossible: new and selected poems 1974-2004*, pub. Bloodaxe Books.
Larkin, Philip *The Trees*	Reproduced by kind permission of Faber & Faber Ltd.	*Collected Poems*, pub. Faber & Faber, 1988.
Lewis, Clive Staples *The Future of Forestry*	Copyright © C. S. Lewis Pte. Ltd. Extract reprinted by permission.	
Lindop, Grevel *Scattering the Ashes*	Reproduced by kind permission of the author and Carcanet Press Ltd.	*Playing with fire*, pub. Carcanet Press, 2006.
Longley, Michael *Two Pheasants*	Reproduced by kind permission of the author and The Random House Group Ltd.	*Collected Poems*, pub. Jonathan Cape, 2006.

MacBeth, George *The Field, Tomorrow*	© George MacBeth 1989. Reproduced by kind permission of Sheil Land Associates Ltd.	*Collected poems 1958-1982*, pub. Hutchinson.
Masefield, John *On Eastnor Knoll* *Tewkesbury Road*	Reproduced by kind permission of the Society of Authors as the literary representatives of the Estate of Laurence Binyon.	
MacCaig, Norman *Fetching Cows*	Reproduced by kind permission of Polygon, an imprint of Birlinn Ltd (www.birlinn.co.uk).	*The Poems of Norman MacCaig.*
McGough, Roger *Soil* *Trees Cannot Name the Seasons*	Reproduced by kind permission of United Agents (www.unitedagents.co.uk) on behalf of Roger McGough.	'Soil' from *Watchwords* © Roger McGough, 1969, and 'Trees Cannot Name the Seasons' from *Melting into the Foreground* © Roger McGough, 1986.
Mitchell, Adrian *Farm Animals*	Reproduced by kind permission of United Agents on behalf of: The Estate of Adrian Mitchell.	*Heart on the Left (Collected Poems 1953-1985)*, pub. Bloodaxe Books.
Motion, Andrew *London Plane*	Reproduced by kind permission of Faber & Faber Ltd.	*The Cinder Path*, 2009, pub. Faber & Faber.
Muir, Edwin *The Horses*	Reproduced by kind permission of Faber & Faber Ltd.	*Edwin Muir Selected Poems* edited by Mick Imlah, pub. Faber & Faber, 2008.
Nelson, Geoffrey Kenneth *Muckspreading*	The editors have been unsuccessful in tracing right(s) holders.	Sourced from *The Listening Earth*, pub. Merlin Unwin Books 2003.
Nicholson, Norman *Five Rivers*	Reproduced by kind permission of David Higham Associates Limited.	*Collected poems*, pub. Faber & Faber, 1994.
Patten, Brian *In Tintagel Graveyard* *Frogs in the Wood*	Copyright © Brian Patten. Reproduced by kind permission of the author c/o Rogers, Coleridge & White Ltd., 20 Powis Mews, London W11 1JN.	*Selected Poems* by Brian Patten, and *The Listening Earth* pub. Merlin Unwin.
Petrucci, Mario *Assembling a Tree*	Reproduced by kind permission of the author. Copyright © Mario Petrucci 2008.	First published in *The Green Poetry Pack*, part of the Poetry Society's educational resource, The Ecopoetry Study Packs (www.poetry society.org.uk/content/ education/poetryclass/ news).

Raine, Kathleen *The River*	Reproduced by kind permission of Brian Keeble, Literary Executor, Estate of Kathleen Raine.	*Collected Poems of Kathleen Raine*, pub. Golgonooza Press, 2000.
Sackville-West, Vita *The Land: Winter*	Reproduced with permission of Curtis Brown Group Ltd, London on behalf of the Estate of Vita Sackville-West.	Copyright © Vita Sackville-West 1926.
Shepherd, Michael *The Harvest of the Mind*	Reproduced by kind permission of Michael Shepherd's literary executors.	
Shukman, Henry *Horses at Christmas*	Reproduced by kind permission of The Random House Group Ltd.	*In Doctor No's Garden*, by Henry Shukman, pub. Jonathan Cape.
Simpson, James *Barn Owl*	Reproduced by kind permission of the author.	
Smith, Ken *The Countryside Around Dixton Manor, circa 1715*	Reproduced by kind permission of the author and Bloodaxe Books.	*Shed: poems 1980-2001*, pub. Bloodaxe Books.
Steven, Kenneth *Salmon*	Reproduced by kind permission of the author (www.kennethsteven.co.uk).	*Island: Selected Poems by Kenneth Steven* was published by Saint Andrew Press, 2009.
Stuart, Muriel *The Seed Shop*	Reproduced by kind permission of Persephone Books.	*Gardeners Nightcap*, pub. Persephone Books, 2006. Copies available from the publisher.
Thomas, Dylan *Fern Hill*	Reproduced by kind permission of David Higham Associates Limited.	*The Poems of Dylan Thomas*, pub. Dent, 1971.
Thomas, Ronald Stuart *Cynddylan on a Tractor* *The Welsh Hill Country*	Reproduced by kind permission of The Orion Publishing Group.	*RS Thomas: Collected Poems*, pub. J.M. Dent (an imprint of The Orion Publishing Group), 1993.
Thwaite, Anthony *The Foresters Arms*	Reproduced by kind permission of the author.	*Collected Poems*, pub. Enitharmon Press, 2007.
Williams, Ann *The Beekeeper*	Reproduced by kind permission of the author.	